DEDICATION

To the people and places of the Palmetto State, our adopted home.

· ·

CONTENTS

• •

100

THINGS TO DO IN

CHARLESTON

BEFORE YOU

DIE

WITHDRAWN

• •

LYNN AND CELE SELDON

REEDY PRESS

Library of Congress Control Number: 2017957321

ISBN: 9781681061283

Design by Jill Halpin

All photos, including cover photo, courtesy of the Charleston Area CVB, explorecharleston.com.

Printed in the United States of America
18 19 20 21 22   5 4 3 2

Please note that websites, phone numbers, addresses, and company names are subject to change or cancellation. We did our best to relay the most accurate information available, but due to circumstances beyond our control, please do not hold us liable for misinformation. When exploring new destinations, please do your homework before you go.

Music and Entertainment

• •

• •

Shopping and Fashion

• •

PREFACE

When you visit Charleston, you're sure to hear the story of a wealthy older Charlestonian woman who was once asked why she so seldom traveled. She replied, "My dear, why should I travel when I'm already here?"

It's easy to understand this woman's complacence, because few places on earth can rival Charleston's blend of grace, beauty, history, and tradition. Charleston has a way of charming visitors (and residents), so that they never want to leave.

Charleston is an "old world" city, lovingly preserved and unique among American destinations. In this grand old city, church bells still toll the hours and the rhythmic sounds of horse-drawn carriages join in the melody. You can see the antebellum homes and plantations that echo a lifestyle of the Old South and you can feel and smell the salty sea breeze blowing into the city from beaches of the resort islands nearby. Then, you can taste the delicious fresh seafood and more at one of many renowned Charleston restaurants.

Whether taking a carriage tour, shopping at the popular open-air public market for native sweetgrass baskets, looking for antiques along historic King Street, pursuing plantation life, or combing beautiful beaches, Charleston provides a sensational sensory experience. In the city and out at the plantations and elsewhere in

● ●

the Lowcountry, America's oldest gardens explode with vibrant colors and are a delight, as the scent of the flora is like no other and the vision of the alluring azaleas, roses, and camellias are almost too exquisite to capture on camera.

Charleston is beautiful and aristocratic, where century-old houses peek at visitors behind gates that are alive with Carolina jessamine, the state flower of South Carolina. If you happen to be in Charleston during the spring or fall, some of the oldest and grandest homes and gardens are open to the public.

First-time and veteran visitors, as well as residents exploring their own city, should head to the Charleston Visitor Center at 375 Meeting Street. Here, you'll enjoy a multisensory presentation called "Forever Charleston," and you'll have access to lots of brochures and information, many tour and attraction tickets, and even the regularly departing DASH Trolley.

Charleston is always colorful and forever charming. It's easy to understand why residents (and visitors) never want to leave. They, too, know they're already there.

We had a very hard time narrowing down our list of "100 Things" for Charleston. We'd love to hear about your experiences with our choices and learn other "100 Things" possibilities. Find us on Facebook and Twitter @SeldonInk and tag your own #100ThingsCharleston adventures.

Lynn & Cele Seldon

ACKNOWLEDGMENTS

When Charleston friends and veteran visitors learned about this book, ideas for what to include came pouring into our inboxes and phones. We could not have written the book without the help of dozens of people. You know who you are . . . thank you!

Everyone we contacted at restaurants, hotels, attractions, and elsewhere was as helpful and charming as possible—we expected nothing less from such a gracious city. This book is a love letter to all of them and to everyone who makes visiting Charleston—or living here—one of the world's most wonderful experiences.

We'd especially like to thank Helen Hill and her incredible team at the Charleston Area Convention & Visitors Bureau, as well as everyone at the South Carolina Department of Parks, Recreation & Tourism.

FOOD AND DRINK

TAKE A BITE OUT OF CHARLESTON
AT THE CHARLESTON WINE + FOOD FESTIVAL

One of the tastiest and most efficient ways to take a big bite out of the Charleston food and drink scene is at the Charleston Wine + Food Festival. Starting on Wednesday and running through Sunday, it's held the first weekend in March (though it may begin in late February). Annual highlights of more than one hundred possibilities include opening night, highlighting the cuisine of more than thirty-five local chefs; the Culinary Village in Marion Square (great for sampling lots of varied foods and beverages); many signature dinners pairing local and visiting chefs with wineries and wines or other beverages; seminars on wine and other beverages; Shucked (an oyster roast); and much more. Special packages (including multiple event tickets, accommodations, and more) can be a bargain.

843-727-9998
charlestonwineandfood.com

TIP
Sunday's Culinary Village is typically less crowded, with shorter tasting lines. Locals also get a great discount on Sunday's Village ticket.

OTHER GREAT WAYS TO TAKE A BITE (OR GULP) OUT OF CHARLESTON

Charleston Restaurant Week
(January & September)
843-853-8000
charlestonrestaurantassociation.com

Lowcountry Oyster Festival
(January)
1235 Long Point Rd. (Boone Hall Plantation)
Mount Pleasant, 843-853-8000
charlestonrestaurantassociation.com

Charleston Beer Garden
(May)
40 Patriots Point Rd. (Patriots Point)
Mount Pleasant, 843-747-2273
charlestonbeergarden.com

Charleston Beer Week
(September)
charlestonbeerweek.com

Oktoberfest Charleston
(October)
405 King St. (St. Matthew's Lutheran Church)
843-723-1611
oktoberfestcharleston.com

EAT SHRIMP AND GRITS
AT SLIGHTLY NORTH OF BROAD (SNOB)

Along with she-crab soup, few dishes say Charleston and the Lowcountry more than shrimp and grits. There are dozens of tasty versions found in all types of restaurants throughout the Charleston area, but possibly none are more adored than the shrimp and grits at Slightly North of Broad (known as "SNOB" by veteran visitors), which is located a few blocks north of Broad Street. Created decades ago by beloved chef Frank Lee (he still serves as Chef Emeritus), his recipe is generally traditional yet creative, and oh so tasty. The delectable and picture-perfect dish features juicy shrimp, creamy stone-ground Geechee Boy grits, country ham, house sausage, garlic, tomatoes, and lots of love from SNOB's current chefs. The shrimp and grits—and SNOB—are simply Charleston classics.

192 E Bay St., 843-723-3424
snobcharleston.com

TIP
SNOB remains extremely popular and scoring a reservation for lunch is easier than one for dinner. And shrimp and grits is on the lunch menu.

EAT UP CHARLESTON
ON A CULINARY TOUR

Charleston's famed food scene is easily explored through one or more varied culinary tours with knowledgeable guides, and a growing list of tour options draws lots of hungry repeat visitors. Charleston Culinary Tours has an array of two-and-a-half- to three-hour options, with tasty possibilities including the Downtown Charleston Culinary Tour, the Upper King Street Culinary Tour, the Chef's Kitchen Tour, the Mixology Tour, and the Farm-to-Table Experience. Owned and operated by Bulldog Tours (a company that has many other Charleston tour options), Charleston Food Tours features many other choices, including Taste of the Lowcountry, Savor the Flavors of Charleston, Savor the Flavors of Upper King, Chef's Kitchen Tour, Celebrity Chef Experience, and the popular Dessert Tour. They run two to two and a half hours.

Charleston Culinary Tours
843-259-2966
charlestonculinarytours.com

Charleston Food Tours
843-727-1100
charlestonfoodtours.com

TIP
Don't eat before a culinary tour in Charleston, where they're as hospitable with samples as they are with smiles.

BASK
IN THE BIVALVE CULTURE

Oysters are synonymous with Charleston's culinary culture and can be found raw and roasted in every nook and cranny all year long (even in months without an "r"). Slurp back raw oysters from the Chesapeake Bay, Gulf Coast, or South Carolina's ACE Basin at the Darling Oyster Bar's classic shucking station overlooking bustling King Street. Sample the Virginia farm-raised cultured oysters at Rappahannock Oyster Bar. Try some of the world's best oysters with an oyster platter at the Ordinary. Or dive into a mess of roasted oysters at everyone's favorite seafood shack at Bowens Island Restaurant or the many community and civic oyster roasts throughout the fall and winter. Don't miss the mother-lode oyster event every January at the annual Lowcountry Oyster Festival—where they serve up more than eighty thousand pounds.

The Darling Oyster Bar
513 King St., 843-641-0821, thedarling.com

Rappahannock Oyster Bar
701 E Bay St., 843-576-4693, rroysters.com

The Ordinary
544 King St., 843-414-7060, eattheordinary.com

Bowens Island Restaurant
1870 Bowens Island Rd., 843-795-2757, bowensisland.biz

Lowcountry Oyster Festival, Boone Hall Plantation
1235 Long Point Rd., Mount Pleasant
charlestonrestaurantassociation.com

SPOON UP SOME SHE-CRAB SOUP
AT 82 QUEEN

Like shrimp and grits, many think of she-crab soup as a classic Charleston dish. Though versions of it can be traced to Scottish settlers in the South as early as the 1700s, legend has it that today's Charleston she-crab soup was created by Mayor Goodwyn Rhett's butler at the John Rutledge House during one of several visits by President William Howard Taft. Today, varied recipes can be enjoyed at many Charleston-area restaurants, but many longtime residents swear by the she-crab soup and historic setting served up at 82 Queen. There's lots of butter and cream involved, but it's the crab roe (eggs), crab meat, fish stock, sherry, and whipped sherry cream that give this dish nearly holy status in the Holy City.

82 Queen St., 843-723-7591
82queen.com

EXTRA CREDIT
Whether or not she-crab soup was invented for a visiting president at the John Rutledge House (116 Broad St.), it remains a presidential place to stay. johnrutledgehouseinn.com

DRINK A PBR
AT THE RECOVERY ROOM

Officially known as the Recovery Room Tavern, this neighborhood dive bar is also beloved as the nation's top seller of twelve-ounce Pabst Blue Ribbon cans. The PBRs are rapidly and frequently retrieved for loyal patrons from a barrel full of ice water from the time the doors open until they close every day. A daily happy hour from 4 p.m. to 8 p.m. makes already-cheap PBRs and more even less expensive, while live music, DJs, bocce, pool, foosball, sports on TV, lots of other beers on draft, spirits, cocktails, and popular bar food draw a diverse crowd. The Tater Tot Tachos™, made with a blend of Monterey jack and cheddar cheese, tomatoes, onions, and green and jalapeño peppers, pair perfectly with an ice-cold can of PBR.

685 King St., 843-727-0999
recoveryroomtavern.com

TAKE A COOKING CLASS
IN THE KITCHEN WITH BOB WAGGONER

Beloved as the longtime chef at Belmond Charleston Place's Charleston Grill from 1997 to 2009, Bob Waggoner now offers often sold-out cooking classes in a contemporary Market Street kitchen and dining space. The two- to three-hour classes feature different menus every night and include convivial cooking instruction, active participation, and a tasty dinner. Waggoner works with local farmers and fishermen to source the freshest food for his classes—preparing, cooking, and serving what he finds "fun and sexy" each week. Popular with individuals, couples, and groups of all kinds, the high-energy classes are enjoyable, entertaining, educational, and oh so edible. Be sure to mention any food allergies when making a reservation for a unique evening.

164-A Market St., 843-619-7529
chefbobwaggoner.com

GO WHOLE HOG
AT RODNEY SCOTT'S WHOLE HOG BBQ

Rodney Scott already had a loyal following at his original whole hog 'cue joint up in Hemingway, South Carolina, but the opening of his Charleston location brought thousands more into his devoted pigpen. Scott and his crew still smoke whole hogs overnight over chopped wood, and you can smell the restaurant blocks before you get to its Upper King address north of downtown. The meat is hand-chopped and served on a sandwich with one side or as a platter with two sides. Scott is serious about his scratch-made sides as well, including hush puppies, coleslaw, baked beans, mac and cheese, greens, and a veggie of the day. Other options at his no-frills joint include BBQ spare ribs, pit-smoked chicken, a rib-eye sandwich, and catfish.

1011 King St., 843-990-9535
rodneyscottsbbq.com

EXTRA CREDIT
There are more than a dozen (and counting) barbecue hot spots in Charleston, and each of them have their own loyal followings, depending on style, flavor, sides, ambience, and more.

SOME OTHER BBQ HOT SPOTS

Home Team BBQ
126 Williman St.
843-225-7427, ext. 4

2209 Middle St.
Sullivan's Island
843-225-7427, ext. 3

1205 Ashley River Rd.
West Ashley
843-225-7427, ext. 2

hometeambbq.com

Jim 'N Nick's Bar-B-Q
4964 Center Pointe Dr.
North Charleston
843-747-3800

1486 Stuart Engals Blvd.
Mount Pleasant
843-375-6509

jimnnicks.com

Lewis Barbecue
464 North Nassau St.
843-805-9500

lewisbarbecue.com

Queology
32-C North Market St.
843-580-2244

192 College Park Rd.
Ladson
843-569-6000

queology.com

Smoke BBQ
487 King St.
843-805-5050

713 Coleman Blvd.
Mount Pleasant
843-936-2027

smokebbq.kitchen

Swig & Swine
1217 Savannah Hwy.
West Ashley
843-225-3805

1990 Old Trolley Rd.
Summerville
843-771-9688

swigandswinebbq.com

FEAST ON STICKY BUN SUNDAYS

Charleston is well known for brunching on the weekends. It's somewhat of a religion. But for another take on the first meal of the day, do like the locals do and head to WildFlour Pastry for Sticky Bun Sundays. Pastry chef Lauren Mitterer thought it would be a great way to bring in the community when she opened her shop in 2010. The concept has stuck. The bakeries are abuzz every Sunday morning when folks come for hot coffee, camaraderie, and those chewy, gooey sticky buns. Served warm and topped with either caramelized pecans and brown sugar or cinnamon and a cream cheese frosting, the buns are only served on Sundays at WildFlour's two locations.

73 Spring St., 843-327-2621
1750 Savannah Highway, 843-990-9391
wildflourpastrycharleston.com

TIP
Head to WildFlour Pastry early on Sundays because it is only open from 8 a.m. until 1 p.m., and it only has the decadent sticky buns until they run out.

HAVE A CUP OF TEA
ON WADMALAW ISLAND

About twenty miles south of Charleston lies Wadmalaw Island and the Charleston Tea Plantation. With its sandy soils, subtropical climate, and average rainfall of fifty-two inches per year, Wadmalaw hosts the perfect conditions for the *Camellia sinensis* tea plant originally brought over from China. Used to produce both black and green teas, this tea plant covers 127 acres of the plantation and is used to create nine different Charleston Tea Plantation brand flavors, including its original American Classic Tea. As part of the Bigelow Tea Company, Charleston Tea Plantation sells its own tea bags, loose tea, bottled teas, and gift items, as well as offering plantation trolley tours, factory tours, and exclusive tours with the founder, tea maker, and tea taster, William Barclay Hall.

6617 Maybank Highway, Wadmalaw Island
843-559-0383
charlestonteaplantation.com

FUN FACT
Charleston Tea Plantation brand tea is the only large- scale commercially grown tea in America. All the teas are made with 100 percent tea grown on the plantation.

DINE AROUND THE WORLD
IN PARK CIRCLE

Park Circle is one of the most up-and-coming neighborhoods in Charleston, and the area has become a dining melting pot. Created as one of South Carolina's first planned communities, this North Charleston community is now host to more than a dozen ethnic and specialty food restaurants. Whether dinner calls for modern Mexican at Mixson Grille, pub grub at sports bar DIG in the Park, pizza at EVO (Extra Virgin Oven), Italian at Fratellos Italian Tavern, or New Orleans fare at LoLA, there is something for everyone. And don't even get us started on the Vietnamese at Lotus, Irish grub at Madra Rua Irish Pub, burgers at Sesame Burger, Mediterranean fare at Stems & Skins, or traditional 'cue at the Barbecue Joint— Park Circle will have you salivating for more.

Mixson Grille
4401 McCarthy St., North Charleston
843-471-1670, mixsongrille.com

DIG in the Park
1049 E Montague Ave., North Charleston
843-225-5201, dighospitality.com

EVO (Extra Virgin Oven)
1075 E Montague Ave., North Charleston
843-225-1796, evopizza.com

Fratellos Italian Tavern
1050 E Montague Ave., North Charleston
843-554-5021, fratellostavern.com

LoLA Low Country Louisiana Seafood Kitchen
4830 O'Hear Ave., North Charleston
843-990-9416, lolaparkcircle.com

Lotus
1070 E Montague Ave., North Charleston
843-225-9240, lotusparkcircle.com

Madra Rua Irish Pub
1034 E Montague Ave., North Charleston
843-554-2522, madraruapub.com

Sesame Burger
4726 Spruill Ave., North Charleston
843-554-4903, sesameburgersandbeer.com

Stems & Skins
1070 E Montague Ave., North Charleston
843-805-4809, stemsandskins.com

The Barbecue Joint
1921 Reynolds Ave., North Charleston
843-747-4567, thebarbequejoint.com

CELEBRATE YOUR FREEDOM WITH A PROHIBITION PINT
AT BLIND TIGER PUB

Blind tigers were all the rage in the late 1800s as temperance legislation was sweeping the nation and Prohibition was around the corner. These illegal bars started popping up in Charleston in 1893, and many of them were located along Broad Street. So it came as no surprise when the Blind Tiger Pub opened nearly one hundred years later in the same location to pay homage to this historic period in Charleston's history. Housed in a building built in 1803—with accompanying ghost tales that you might expect—and having changed owners several times in the past twenty-five years, Blind Tiger Pub serves up elevated pub grub (we're talking smoked wings, chargrilled oysters, and truffle duck sandwiches) and a beer and cocktail list that would make the ghosts of Prohibition proud.

36–38 Broad St., 843-872-6700
blindtigerchs.com

HANG A DOLLAR BILL
AT THE GRIFFON

In a city filled with grace and charm, there still resides a seedier side to Charleston. And in the case of the Griffon, that seedier side has become legendary. Often praised as "unapologetically awesome," "best no-frills watering hole," and "Charleston's greatest dive bar—possibly ever" by publications in the know, the Griffon has been welcoming businessmen, couples, blue-collar tradesmen, the late-night restaurant industry, and visiting families for more than twenty years. And the bar has walls and ceilings of crumpled one-dollar bills to prove it. Focusing on good beers—with sixteen on tap and plenty more by the can and bottle—and cheap food, the Griffon serves up traditional pub grub in a kitschy, convivial atmosphere and makes everyone who enters feel welcome.

18 Vendue Range, 843-723-1700
griffoncharleston.com

HEAD TO BREAKFAST (OR BRUNCH)
AT HOMINY GRILL

Charleston's first James Beard Foundation Award winner, Robert Stehling, and his Hominy Grill hot spot are packed seven days a week from morning to night (except Sundays, when they close mid-afternoon to catch their collective breaths). The lunch and dinner menus are as creative as ever, but the breakfast and brunch menus often lead to lines—including at the little window that serves up Bloody Marys and more while you wait. Veterans have their favorites for every meal, but it's hard to beat Stehling's interpretation of shrimp and grits for breakfast or brunch—with scallions, mushrooms, bacon, and cheesy grits. Breakfast is served from 7:30 a.m. to 11:30 a.m., Monday to Friday, with brunch running 9 a.m. to 3 p.m. on Saturday and Sunday.

207 Rutledge Ave., 843-577-2337
hominygrill.com

EXTRA CREDIT

Located just across Rutledge Avenue from Hominy Grill, the Rutledge Avenue Inn is about as convenient as it gets for heading to Hominy Grill when the line is short—or cooking in when the line is long, thanks to the gourmet kitchens in all of the inn's luxurious condos (plus a cottage). therutledgeavenueinn.com

SEE AND BE SEEN
AT THE DEWBERRY

Charleston's darling hot spot is the Living Room at the Dewberry. Located in the lobby of this hip hotel on Marion Square, the Living Room is dressed in mid-century furnishings, a hand-selected reading library, and a magnificent brass bar that evokes the Southern hospitality and grace of a Charleston home. Stop in for a morning coffee or afternoon cocktail and commune with Charleston's movers and shakers. Or grab a meal in Henrietta's, a traditional French brasserie—with a touch of Southern—serving breakfast, lunch, and dinner as well as a sumptuous weekend brunch. And don't miss Fieldshop, two boutiques off the lobby that feature a collection of "Hunt" masculine lifestyle products and "Gather" feminine luxury items, curated by the folks at Garden & Gun®.

334 Meeting St., 843-558-8000
thedewberrycharleston.com

GET CRABBY

Crabs are a South Carolina delicacy, and the waters around Charleston are teeming with them. Make your own feast by picking up some chicken necks and string and dropping a line in any of the Lowcountry waterways to snag your own and steam 'em up. If it's softshell season—usually March and April—head to one of the area seafood purveyors, like Mt. Pleasant Seafood on Shem Creek or Crosby's Fish & Shrimp on Folly Beach and pick up some softies to fry up at home. If you prefer someone else to do the cooking, check out one of the area's restaurants that feature these beauties, like the Ordinary, the Grocery, or Edmund's Oast. Or try a true Charleston specialty with she-crab soup at 82 Queen or High Cotton.

Mt. Pleasant Seafood
1402 Shrimp Boat Lane, Mount Pleasant
843-884-4122
mtpleasantseafood.com

Crosby's Fish & Shrimp Co.
2223 Folly Rd., 843-795-4049
crosbysfishshrimp.com

The Ordinary
544 King St., 843-414-7060
eattheordinary.com

The Grocery
4 Cannon St., 843-302-8825
thegrocerycharleston.com

Edmund's Oast
1081 Morrison Dr., 843-727-1145
edmundsoast.com

82 Queen
82 Queen St., 843-723-7591
82queen.com

High Cotton
199 E Bay St., 843-724-3815
highcottoncharleston.com

CAPTURE FIREFLIES
ON A TIPSY TOUR

We're not talking lightning bugs here. We're talking spirits that are distilled on Wadmalaw Island, thirty miles south of Charleston in the middle of the Lowcountry. Take a Tipsy Tour with Sea Island Tours to the home of Firefly Distillery—makers of the original sweet tea vodka—and the adjacent Deep Water Vineyard, Charleston's only domestic winery and vineyard. The tour starts with a tasting of five wines paired with a fruit and cheese tray. Then move on to the dark side with a tasting of your choice of six of Firefly's spirits, including its flagship vodka, whiskies, moonshines, and craft liqueurs. Lastly, head to Low Tide Brewing on Johns Island for a flight of handcrafted beers. The best part? Tipsy Tours will pick you up and drop you off at the Charleston Visitor Center.

Tipsy Tour with Sea Island Tours
843-559-6867, seaislandtours.com/tipsytour

Firefly Distillery
6775 Bears Bluff Rd., Wadmalaw Island, 843-557-1405
fireflyspirits.com

Deep Water Vineyard
6775 Bears Bluff Rd., Wadmalaw Island, 843-559-6867
deepwatervineyard.com

Low Tide Brewing
2863 Maybank Highway, Johns Island, 843-501-7570
lowtidebrewing.com

ATTEND A GOSPEL BRUNCH
IN THE HOLY CITY

With so many historic churches in the Holy City, attending Sunday services is a big thing. But Sunday brunch is almost bigger. Some would even say it's a religion. And the Sunday gospel brunch at Hall's Chophouse is the consummate place to worship. The local gospel choir, the Plantation Singers, performs every Sunday, and its soulful sounds and classic Southern hymns help to preserve the spiritual and sacred music of the Gullah community and the Lowcountry. And it's the perfect accompaniment to Hall's upscale and refined Southern brunch, featuring classics like she-crab soup, fried green tomatoes, oysters Rockefeller, creative omelets, varied Benedicts, shrimp and grits, and Southern sweet baked potato pancakes—all of it served up with some of the most gracious hospitality in all of Charleston.

434 King St., 843-727-0090
hallschophouse.com

SEE CHARLESTON
FROM A BIRD'S-EYE VIEW

There's no better way to view the stunning skyline of Charleston—not to mention the insane Lowcountry sunsets—than from a rooftop. That's why downtown is loaded with spectacular rooftop bars where you can enjoy a cocktail or meal with a view. Some of the best options include the views of Charleston Harbor from Burwell's Stone Fire Grill, overlooking Marion Square at Carolina Ale House, creative cocktails at the Cocktail Club, dancing the night away at Henry's Rooftop, cold brews at Revelry Brewing, and the ever-popular and often-packed Stars Rooftop. Several area hotels boast some of the best rooftops, like the fairy-tale-esque Élevé in the Grand Bohemian, the swanky Pavilion Bar at Market Pavilion, the Rooftop at the Vendue, and the Watch at the Restoration.

Burwell's Stone Fire Grill
14 N Market St., 843-737-8700
burwellscharleston.com

Carolina Ale House
145 Calhoun St., 843-805-7020
carolinaalehouse.com

The Cocktail Club
479 King St., 843-724-9411
thecocktailclubcharleston.com

Henry's Rooftop & Deck
54 N Market St., 843-723-4363
henryshousecharleston.com

Revelry Brewing
10 Conroy St., 843-203-6194
revelrybrewingco.com

Stars Rooftop
495 King St., 843-577-0100
starsrestaurant.com

Élevé French Kitchen & Lounge
55 Wentworth St., 843-724-4144
grandbohemiancharleston.com

Pavilion Bar at Market Pavilion
225 E Bay St., 843-723-0500
marketpavilion.com

The Rooftop at the Vendue
19 Vendue Range, 843-577-7970
thevendue.com

The Watch Rooftop Kitchen and Spirits
75 Wentworth St., 877-221-7202
therestorationhotel.com

DRINK IN HISTORY
ON THE ORIGINAL PUB TOUR

Listen to tales of bootleggers, ghosts, presidents, and pirates as you explore Charleston's history through its most historic taverns and pubs with the Original Pub & Brewery Tours of Charleston. The company offers two walking tour options—the Original Pub Tour or the Upper King Street Pub Crawl—that cover three to five pubs in an easy-walking, two-and-a-half-hour tour, with samples of local craft brews and traditional appetizers. They also feature a healthy dose of Charleston's history from the historic taverns and former speakeasies to rooftop pubs and breweries. Hosted by beer brewers with a passion for history, these small group outings are a great way to drink in the city. Also on offer are Bachelorette Pub Crawls, Haunted Pub Crawls throughout the month of October, and Brewery Bus Tours.

843-577-5535
pubtourcharleston.com

ASIAN MEETS SOUTHERN
AT XIAO BAO BISCUIT

Situated in a former gas station, Xiao Bao Biscuit consistently receives rave reviews for its continent-crossing Asian cuisine. The popular Okonomiyaki cabbage pancakes—the chef learned to make them while working on a Japanese farm for six weeks—have been on the menu from the day it opened. Made with cabbage, scallions, mayonnaise, and sweet soy and hot sauces, they're available for lunch or dinner year-round. Seasonal dishes using local vegetables and seafood, as well as classic Asian takes and plenty of vegetarian options, also attract lots of repeat visitors after their introduction to Xiao Bao Biscuit's magic through the pancakes. The small bar, with a large opening into the kitchen, is a convivial spot for single diners and enjoying creative cocktails.

224 Rutledge Ave.
xiaobaobiscuit.com

EXTRA CREDIT
The team that brought Xiao Bao Biscuit to Charleston also runs Tu (430 Meeting Street), which stretches beyond Asia with creative cuisines from around the world.
tu-charleston.com

EAT SOME SOUL FOOD
AT BERTHA'S KITCHEN

Knighted an "America's Classic" by the James Beard Foundation (as was Charleston's Bowens Island Restaurant), Bertha's Kitchen is most definitely a Charleston-area soul food classic. Albertha Grant opened Bertha's in 1981, and it now belongs to her three daughters, with help from lots of cousins and other family members. Situated in a turquoise-painted building up Meeting Street Road in North Charleston, the Bertha's cafeteria-style meat 'n' three experience features different specials every day. However, daily mainstays like mouthwatering fried chicken, fried whiting, and fried pork chops are almost always on offer—until they're gone for the day. Plus, Southern sides like sweet cornbread, boiled cabbage, mac and cheese, greens, okra soup, and more remain part of the heart and soul of this Southern soul food landmark.

2332 Meeting St., North Charleston
843-554-6519

TIP
Bertha's Kitchen opens at 11 a.m. and closes at 6 p.m., Monday to Thursday. Go early or late to avoid the frequent lunchtime lines.

OTHER TASTY SOUL FOOD SPOTS

Eastside Soul Food
46A America St., 843-973-3100

Martha Lou's Kitchen
1068 Morrison Dr., 843-577-9583
marthalouskitchen.com

Hannibal's Soul Kitchen
15 Blake St., 843-722-2256
hannibalkitchen.com

My Three Sons
1910 E Montague Ave., North Charleston
843-202-0189
mythreesonsofcharleston.com

Nana's Seafood & Soul
176 Line St., 843-937-0002

Workmen's Café
1837 Grimball Rd., 843-406-0120

BITE INTO A BODACIOUS BURGER

It's a daunting task to pick your favorite burger. It's sort of like picking your favorite child. But there are a handful of spots that are killing it in the Charleston burger wars. Little Jack's brisket-and-chuck Tavern Burger is available as a one-patty snack or a two-patty sandwich. Heck, they even have it on the dessert menu. Chef Sean Brock's burger with ground bacon at Husk has almost reached cult status. The folks at Ted's Butcherblock cut and grind their meat in house so you know it's fresh. And they grill up a new Ultimate Burger every Saturday on a Big Green Egg out front. Although the burger at classic dive Tattooed Moose is fantastic, it's really a side order of the duck fat fries that seals the deal.

Little Jack's Tavern
710 King St., 843-531-6868
littlejackstavern.com

Husk
76 Queen St., 843-577-2500
huskrestaurant.com

Ted's Butcherblock
334 E Bay St., 843-577-0094
tedsbutcherblock.com

Tattooed Moose
1137 Morrison Dr., 843-277-2990
tattooedmoose.com

DRINK UP A PUNCH BOWL
AT THE ROYAL AMERICAN

Known as a top spot to catch a busy schedule of live music and more for little dough, the Royal American is also known for its "punch bowls." Mixed with a choice of bourbon, rum, or vodka, the punch bowls feature a full thirty-two ounces of punch, served over crushed ice in a free souvenir stadium cup and shake straw. They somehow seem to make the music sound even better. Originally the Ole Charleston Forge metalworking company, the Royal American features live music on most nights and is open seven nights a week (and starting at noon on Saturdays and Sundays). The concert schedule and resulting crowds are quite eclectic. Ranging from rock to reggae to heavy metal and many genre-bending bands, the shows here are often a punch to the ears.

970 Morrison Dr., 843-817-6925
theroyalamerican.com

EXTRA CREDIT
The Royal American is also known for its food, including pickled shrimp, house made chili, and tasty sandwiches (muffuletta, fried bologna, patty melt, and more). Everything pairs perfectly with a punch bowl or a cold beer from the long list.

HAVE A PINT
IN CHARLESTON'S OLDEST BREWERY

Paying homage to the original Old Palmetto Brewing Company that satisfied Charleston's thirst for beer from the mid-1800s through 1913, Palmetto Brewing Company is the oldest microbrewery in Charleston—it opened in 1993—and the first area brewery to open since Prohibition. Its core beers include an amber, two IPAs, and a Pilsner, but it's the specialty and seasonal brews like Brosé Shandy and Island Wit Witbier that really set Palmetto apart. So does its tasting room. Featuring brewery tours, free Friday night concerts, and an uber-cool loading dock beer garden, it's the perfect place downtown to enjoy a few pints and kick back. And for the guys, don't miss the men's room, where you can pee into a recycled keg—otherwise known as a kegurinator.

289 Huger St., 843-937-0903
palmettobrewery.com

TIP
There are more than twenty breweries in the greater Charleston area. If you are looking to go further afield than downtown, be sure to check out the complete Charleston Brewery List at charlestonbrewerylist.com.

OTHER DOWNTOWN BREWERIES

Cooper River Brewing
2201-B Mechanic St., 843-405-7979
cooperriverbrewing.com

Edmund's Oast Brewing Co.
1505 King St., 843-718-3224
edmundsoast.com

Fatty's Beer Works
1436 Meeting St., 843-974-5330
fattysbeerworks.com

Lofi Brewing
2038 Meeting St., 828-582-2175
lofibrewing.com

Revelry Brewing
10 Conroy St., 843-203-6194
revelrybrewingco.com

SPLURGE ON A SEAN BROCK–CREATED TASTING MENU
AT MCCRADY'S RESTAURANT

The tasting-menu-only experience at McCrady's Restaurant is like a love letter to Charleston from James Beard Foundation Award winner Sean Brock. It's a twenty-two-seat concept with two seatings a night, and it features more than a dozen ever-changing small dishes, wine pairings, occasional caviar add-ons, and more. It's a relatively expensive evening by almost any standard, but dishes like the "beet leather bark" with cocoa and lime, various uses of aged beef and Southern sides, and multiple colorful desserts make it a bucket list evening for fans of Sean Brock and contemporary Southern cuisine with deep-reaching roots. Kitchen bar and traditional table seating, an open kitchen, and a team of chefs also combine to make for a memorable Charleston evening unlike any other.

McCrady's Restaurant, 2 Unity Alley, 843-577-0025
mccradysrestaurant.com

OTHER SEAN BROCK-DRIVEN CHARLESTON EXPERIENCES

McCrady's Tavern, 2 Unity Alley, 843-577-0025, mccradystavern.com
Husk Restaurant, 76 Queen St., 843-577-2500, huskrestaurant.com
The Bar at Husk, 76 Queen St., 843-577-2500, huskresturant.com
Minero, 153B E Bay St., 843-789-2241, minerorestaurant.com

ENJOY SUNDAY BRUNCH SEVEN DAYS A WEEK
AT POOGAN'S PORCH

Serving brunch seven days a week in a classic Charleston setting inside and out, Poogan's Porch attracts lots of locals and tourists alike. The long list of brunch starters includes she-crab soup, fried green tomatoes, biscuits and gravy, and mac and cheese with country ham and aged smoked gouda. Brunch entrée possibilities include a pimiento cheese BLT, shrimp and grits, Lowcountry omelet (with pimiento cheese, country ham, and burnt peppers), pulled pork Benedict, and chicken and waffles. For the chicken and waffles—which has become a Southern Sunday brunch tradition—Poogan's uses Springer Mountain Farms all-natural chicken breast with sweet potato waffles, sorghum butter, and maple syrup. The bread pudding just might be the perfect ending to Sunday brunch—any day of the week.

72 Queen St., 843-577-2337
poogansporch.com

EXTRA CREDIT
This is also a great place to try the popular Charleston Mix Bloody Mary mixture, which can be found in more than a dozen restaurants in Charleston. Poogan's Porch uses Charleston-bred Dixie Black Pepper Vodka and pickled okra to spice it up a notch. charlestonmix.com.

EAT YOUR VEGGIES (AND MORE)
AT THE CHARLESTON
FARMERS MARKET

Founded in 1988 and managed by the Charleston Office of Cultural Affairs, the Charleston Farmers Market has grown into a Saturday city tradition that now includes more than one hundred varied vendors and other participants. It's open 8 a.m. to 2 p.m. from early April to late November, plus select Sundays during Spoleto Festival USA/Piccolo Spoleto and Saturdays and Sundays in December for the Holiday Market. The Charleston Farmers Market features lots of local produce, plants, herbs, cut flowers, meats, breakfast and lunch vendors, coffee purveyors, live music, juried arts and crafts from local artisans, and more. Locals shop for the week while there, as do visitors with accommodations featuring kitchens. Visitors also enjoy finding tasty treats and more as souvenirs or gifts.

329 Meeting St. (Marion Square), 843-724-7305
charlestonfarmersmarket.com

EXTRA CREDIT
Charleston's Office of Cultural Affairs also manages the West Ashley Farmers Market in Ackerman Park (55 Sycamore Ave., West Ashley), which is open 2 p.m. to 7 p.m. on Wednesdays from mid-April to early October.

OTHER AREA FARMERS MARKETS TO EAT YOUR VEGGIES (AND MORE)

Folly Beach Farmers Market
55 Center St. (Folly River Park), Folly Beach
843-588-2447, visitfolly.com

Daniel Island Farmers Market
860 Island Park Dr., Daniel Island, 843-971-9200
danielisland.com

Hanahan Family Farmers Market
1061 Eagle Landing Rd., Hanahan, 843-408-7068
hanahanfamilyfarmersmarket.com

Isle of Palms Farmers Market
1 14th Ave. (Isle of Palms County Park)
Isle of Palms, 843-886-6428, iop.net

Johns Island Farmers Market
2024 Academy Rd. (Charleston Collegiate School), Johns Island
843-830-0886, johnsislandfarmersmarket.com

Mount Pleasant Farmers Market
645 Coleman Blvd. (Moultrie Middle School)
Mount Pleasant, 843-884-8517
experiencemountpleasant.com

North Charleston Farmers Market
4800 Park Cir., North Charleston, 843-740-5853
northcharleston.org

Pacific Box & Crate Farmers Market
1503 King St., 843-996-4500
workshopcharleston.com

Sullivan's Island Farmers' Market
1921 I'On Ave., Sullivan's Island, 843-883-5744
sullivansisland-sc.com

SHARE (OR DEVOUR) A SLICE OF COCONUT CAKE
AT PENINSULA GRILL

On the menu since Valentine's Day, 1997, the twelve-layer Peninsula Grill Ultimate Coconut Cake® is another Charleston classic. The five-inch-tall, twenty-five-pound cake is actually two cakes cut into three layers each, with fluffy filling, cream cheese icing, and toasted coconut pressed into its sides, delivering decadent bites without being too sweet or coconut-y. A huge slice is one-sixteenth of the cake, but whole coconut cakes are also very popular Charleston souvenirs (and typically cut into many more slices). Along with starting the evening in the restaurant's intimate Champagne Bar, a slice of coconut cake provides the perfect ending to a meal at Peninsula Grill—which features equally exquisite takes on other Charleston classics and more in a classy Lowcountry setting.

112 North Market St., 843-723-0700
peninsulagrill.com

TIP
Many may not know that Peninsula Grill actually ships whole coconut cakes to loyal fans near and far.

ITALIAN MEETS SOUTHERN
AT WILD OLIVE

Wild Olive's Jacques Larsen is a transplanted Frenchman with the heart and stomach of a Southerner—and an Italian. Located out on Johns Island west of Charleston, Wild Olive is like a trip to the Tuscan countryside, but just minutes from downtown. Starters to share can include the house-cured salumi with mozzarella, caponata, and chicken liver rustica crostini, but it's Larsen's pastas that keep fans returning—including his light-as-a-pillow and mouthwatering ricotta and goat cheese gnocchi. Regulars also rave about the side dishes, as well as the wine list—which is almost exclusively Italian. With several intimate yet lively dining areas, this Italian meets Southern destination restaurant is a place to linger with fellow lovers of good food and company.

2867 Maybank Hwy., 843-737-4177
wildoliverestaurant.com

EXTRA CREDIT
Though definitely a different experience, Larsen's other Italian-leaning option, the Obstinate Daughter (2063 Middle Street, Sullivan's Island), also features incredible pastas, pizzas, and more. It's located a block from the beach on Sullivan's Island.
theobstinatedaughter.com

MUSIC AND ENTERTAINMENT

SEE A PERFORMANCE
AT THE HISTORIC DOCK
STREET THEATRE

Charleston's original Dock Street Theatre at the corner of Church Street and Dock Street (now known as Queen Street) opened in 1736 with a performance of *The Recruiting Officer* and was the first building in America built exclusively to be used for theatrical productions. After being destroyed in the Great Fire of 1740, it reopened in 1809 as the Planter's Hotel and—after falling into disrepair after the Civil War—was converted back into a theater and reopened in 1937. Modeled after eighteenth-century London playhouses, the theater's stage house and auditorium were built in the hotel's courtyard. Another renovation in 2010 brought the historic theater into the twenty-first century, and it now houses many of the city's finest cultural productions including Spoleto Festival USA and Charleston Stage, the resident professional theater group.

135 Church St., 843-577-7183
www.charlestonstage.com

OTHER PERFORMING ARTS VENUES

34 West
200 Meeting St., 843-901-9343
34west.org

Black Fedora
164 Church St., 843-937-6453
charlestonmysteries.com

Charleston Performing Arts Center
873 Folly Rd., James Island, 843-991-5582
charlestonperformingarts.org

North Charleston Performing Arts Center
5001 Coliseum Dr., North Charleston, 843-529-5000
northcharlestoncoliseumpac.com

Theater 99
280 Meeting St., 843-853-6687
theatre99.com

Woolfe Street Playhouse
34 Woolfe St., 843-856-1579
woolfestreetplayhouse.com

GO WILD AT THE
SOUTHEASTERN WILDLIFE EXPOSITION

What started in 1983 as a gathering to commemorate the natural world around us has morphed into a three-day celebration of wildlife and nature that attracts more than five hundred exhibitors and more than forty thousand attendees, making it the largest event of its kind. The Southeastern Wildlife Exposition is held every February in various locations around town and showcases the world of wildlife through fine art exhibits, conservation education, sporting demonstrations, food, drink, and galas. It brings together men and women, animal lovers, sportsmen, conservationists, wildlife experts, and artists and artisans to pay tribute and honor our "wild" world with art auctions, dog aquatic competitions, bird shows, fishing classes and demonstrations, decoy auctions, conservation classes and lectures, chef demos, exhibits, and family activities. Take a walk on the wild side at SEWE.

843-723-1748
sewe.com

TIP
With so many events, activities, and wildlife art to view all over town, consider purchasing a three-day general admission ticket and take your time enjoying and participating in all the festivities.

DRIVE ON OVER
TO CARS & COFFEE

Generally held every Saturday morning year-round, Cars & Coffee has become quite the Charleston-area tradition. Beginning around 8 a.m. or so at the Mount Pleasant Towne Centre in front of Atlanta Bread Company, dozens of car and motorcycle enthusiasts converge on the area with—and without—their rides. The free casual event welcomes everyone and every kind of vehicle—from classics to exotics and everything in between. Early morning car gatherings are a national phenomenon, including a website (usa.carsandcoffee.info) mapping regular events. Thanks to the varied backgrounds of area residents, the depth and breadth of vehicles on any given Saturday is worth the trip to this particular Cars & Coffee. It usually ends about 10 a.m. or so, though enthusiasts are known to linger over the cars—and coffee.

1712 Towne Centre Way, Mount Pleasant, 843-216-9900
mtpleasanttownecentre.com

EXTRA CREDIT
There's also a smaller Cars & Coffee held out on Kiawah Island at Freshfields (165 Village Green Lane. It's on the third Saturday of every month (9 a.m. to 11 a.m.), except April, with coffee and breakfast available for purchase at Java Java.
freshfields.com

UNLEASH YOUR INNER FASHIONISTA

Every March, emerging designers and model talent across the East Coast descend for Charleston Fashion Week under the tents at Marion Square. This five-night multimedia fashion event showcases the collections of emerging designers, nationally renowned designer runway shows, alluring on-site and citywide activities, shopping extravaganzas, glittering after-parties, and so much more to help increase brand awareness and raise funds for local charities. Events include emerging designer competitions, Rock the Runway competitions to showcase up-and-coming modeling talent, shopping in style lounges, backstage hair and makeup opportunities, and other events to strut your inner fashionista. Retail stores around town get in on the action, with extended hours, discounted merchandise, promotional events, sip and strolls, happy hours, and high-fashion celebrations.

charlestonfashionweek.com

SUPPORT THE LOCAL BOY DOING GOOD

Local rocker Darius Rucker has been performing in his hometown since his days with Hootie & the Blowfish. Now a solo country-crossover performer, Darius is still doing good through his Hootie & the Blowfish Foundation. Established in 2000, this private nonprofit organization supports charities that are near and dear to its heart with a variety of philanthropy efforts. Much of its fundraising comes from Hootie's Homegrown Roundup, an event every August benefiting the children of the Charleston County School District. The two-pronged event includes a two-day concert and reunion of the original members of the band at Volvo Car Stadium on Daniel Island. The foundation also hosts the Hootie's Back-to-School Roundup, where area students receive haircuts, dental exams, and a bookbag full of school supplies to get a jump start on the school year.

hootie.com

JAM
AT LIVE MUSIC VENUES

Live music abounds at music venues featuring rock, country, bluegrass, jazz, and everything in between. The Music Farm has been bringing homegrown acts and nationally touring bands to the heart of Upper King's entertainment district for more than two decades. Charleston Music Hall is considered by many to be one of the Holy City's most intimate music venues. Or catch live jazz seven nights a week at the ever-elegant Charleston Grill in Belmond Charleston Place. Over on James Island, the Pour House is a local's favorite, with live music six nights a week on the main stage and on the back deck. And you can't go wrong with the lively waterfront venue at the Windjammer on Isle of Palms, featuring live music at one of the city's best beaches.

Most shows require advance tickets, so call ahead or go online.

Music Farm, 32 Ann St., 843-577-6989, musicfarm.com

Charleston Music Hall, 37 John St., 843-853-2252
charlestonmusichall.com

Charleston Grill, 224 King St., 843-577-4522
charlestongrill.com

Pour House, 1977 Maybank Hwy., 843-571-4343
charlestonpourhouse.com

The Windjammer, 1008 Ocean Blvd., Isle of Palms, 866-540-3548
the-windjammer.com

CATCH FREE (OR CHEAP) MUSIC
WITH THE CHARLESTON COMMUNITY BAND

When Darius Rucker calls Charleston home, you know it's a music-loving town. But music lovers in the know also know you don't have to always spend big bucks to catch some great live music. The Charleston Community Band plays a limited schedule of shows each year, including Holiday shows and concerts with the group's smaller jazz ensemble. The music and instruments are varied, in that in-season weekly rehearsals are open to all who bring an instrument and have something unique to add to the ensemble. Members (typically thirty-plus) are expected to attend practices and dress rehearsals and know and practice upcoming music for concerts—and this certainly shows at the well-attended and well-played performances. Admission is free to most concerts, but donations are graciously accepted.

charlestoncommunityband.org

EXPLORE CHARLESTON
THROUGH ITS HOMES AND GARDENS

The architecture and gardens of Charleston are a visual example of her ubiquitous Southern hospitality, and there is no better way to explore both than through a house and garden tour. The Historic Charleston Foundation Festival of Houses and Gardens makes it possible to tour more than 150 private residences and lush gardens during peak blooming season. Tours feature many homes each day—dating back to the eighteenth century through the antebellum and Victorian eras to the twentieth century—across a variety of neighborhoods to give a glimpse of what makes Charleston so special. Other events during the festival include history walking tours, plantation tours, luncheons and other culinary events, concerts and musical events, and the Charleston Antiques Show.

historiccharleston.org

EXTRA CREDIT

If you prefer fall weather and lack of crowds, the Preservation Society of Charleston Fall Tours of Homes, History & Architecture is a monthlong celebration with self-guided tours of private homes and gardens; back of the house, photography, and preservation behind-the-scenes tours; curated architectural tours and walks; ironwork walking tours; and more to give you an up-close and personal view of Charleston's history.

preservationsociety.org/falltours

If you can't get enough of flowers, the spring Garden Club of Charleston Annual House & Garden Tour spends two days touring some of the most beautiful homes in the historic district, and each house is magnificently adorned with stunning floral arrangements created by the members of the Garden Club of Charleston.

thegardenclubofcharleston.org/annual-house-and-garden-tour

GET YOUR ART ON
AT THE ARTWALK

For art lovers, the Charleston Gallery Association hosts Artwalks, where enthusiasts and novices alike take to the cobblestoned streets of Charleston, moving from gallery to gallery and soaking in everything from oil painting to photography, sculpture, glassblowing, and more. Held the first Friday each March, May, October, and December from 5 p.m. to 8 p.m., these festive art evenings are free and invite participants to stop by any of the forty-plus participating local art galleries, pick up a gallery map, and stroll at their own pace from place to place. Enjoy complimentary wine and hors d'oeuvres, extended gallery hours, and the opportunity to mingle and chat with the artists themselves along the way as you experience Charleston's burgeoning art scene.

charlestongalleryassociation.com

TIP
Looking for a more immersive art experience? Take a tour with Canvas Charleston. It offers four different tours to introduce you to the scope of Charleston galleries, including Iconic Charleston, Scenic Views, Contemporary, and Behind the Scenes (studio visits).
canvascharleston.com

ENJOY A PERFORMANCE
AT SPOLETO FESTIVAL USA
& PICCOLO SPOLETO

Begun in 1977 as the USA's version of Italy's Festival of Two Worlds in Spoleto, Spoleto Festival USA features seventeen days of widely varied performing arts programs each spring (beginning the Friday before Memorial Day). Offered in historic theaters, churches, outdoor spaces, and elsewhere, the performances encompass all types of music, theater, opera, dance, and more. Now one of the world's top performing arts festivals, Spoleto has hosted more than two hundred world or American premieres featuring renowned performers and emerging artists. There are performances every day, with a concentration of events on weekends. Running over the same seventeen days, Piccolo Spoleto was created by the city's Office of Cultural Affairs in 1979 as a complement to Spoleto Festival USA. Offerings focus more on the Southeast, with tickets generally easier to score.

Spoleto Festival USA
14 George St., 843-722-2764, spoletousa.org

Piccolo Spoleto
75 Calhoun St., Ste. 3800, 843-724-7305, piccolospoleto.com

TIP
Available through the festival's website, Go Spoleto! hotel and ticket packages can offer great savings to those attending multiple events.

REJOICE
IN CHARLESTON'S CULTURAL HERITAGE

Charleston is filled with a cornucopia of cultural heritage, and this diversity is celebrated throughout the year at varied heritage festivals.

Created to promote and preserve the indigenous Gullah/Geechee culture, the Sweetgrass Cultural Arts Festival showcases the foods, music, stories, and artistry of sweetgrass basket making. African American and Caribbean contributions are honored with captivating music, dance, visual arts, and ethnic foods at the MOJA Arts Festival. The Latin American Festival celebrates all things Latin, with amazing performances inspired by culture from around the globe. Charleston becomes Greek every Mother's Day weekend at the Charleston Greek Festival. And the Scottish community struts its stuff at the Scottish Games and Highland Gathering, with Scotch whisky tastings, the black tie (and Highland evening dress) Tartan Ball, piping and drumming, and athletic and dance demonstrations.

Sweetgrass Cultural Arts Festival, sweetgrass.org
MOJA Arts Festival, mojafestival.com
Latin American Festival, charlestoncountyparks.com
Charleston Greek Festival, charlestongreekfestival.com
Scottish Games and Highland Gathering, charlestonscots.org

LIGHT UP THE SEASON
AT THE HOLIDAY FESTIVAL OF LIGHTS

Kick off the holiday season with more than two million twinkling lights at the Holiday Festival of Lights at James Island County Park from mid-November through New Year's Day. Delight in the three-mile driving tour with more than seven hundred dazzling designs. Park your car and explore the fifty-ton holiday sand sculpture, explore behind the scenes of the holiday kingdom on a train ride, or take a stroll through the enchanted forest. Make it a family affair with rides on the Victorian carousel, interacting with lighted trees at Lakeside Lights, or marveling at the giant greeting card display. Enjoy tasty treats at Santa's Sweet Shoppe or the marshmallow roasting pits. And don't forget to visit Santa's Village to get a photo with the big guy himself!

James Island County Park, 871 Riverland Dr., 843-795-4386
holidayfestivaloflights.com

JAM
AT A JAZZ FESTIVAL

It's not surprising that Charleston's jazz festival scene is so lively, thanks to the city's longtime love of the historic American genre. There are now three annual area jazz festivals, and all are unique. January's Charleston Jazz Festival lasts four days and brings together more than one hundred local, regional, and world-renowned musicians in a variety of settings. The possibilities include headline acts, a jazz brunch, late-night shows, and more. Over Labor Day weekend, the Greater Charleston Lowcountry Jazz Festival brings two nights of headline acts to the Charleston Gaillard Center. Shows at the two-day Folly Jazz Festival in October are generally more intimate than the other two options, with a variety of shows taking place in pretty Folly River Park.

Charleston Jazz Festival
843-641-0011
charlestonjazz.com

Greater Charleston Lowcountry Jazz Festival
843-529-5000
lowcountryjazzfest.com

Folly Jazz Festival
843-588-2447
follyjazzfestival.com

LAUGH OUT LOUD
WITH THE HAVE NOTS!

Who doesn't like a good laugh? A night with the *Saturday Night Live*–esque comedy improv group the Have Nots! will have you rolling down the aisles with their side-splitting (and sometimes thought-provoking) brand of humor. The Have Nots! have performed for more than twenty years in more than 1,400 shows in at least seventy locations in the Charleston area. Opening and now making their home in Theatre 99 since 2005, the Have Nots! perform without any scripts, rely heavily on audience suggestions, and perform totally on improvisation. For more laugh riot, don't miss their annual Charleston Comedy Festival and Piccolo Fringe, the rather irreverent comedy festival-cum-theater contribution to the Piccolo Spoleto festivities every spring.

Theatre 99
280 Meeting St., 843-853-6687
theatre99.com

Charleston Comedy Festival
charlestoncomedyfestival.com

Piccolo Fringe
theatre99.com

CHANNEL THE ROMANCE
OF *THE NOTEBOOK*

Nicholas Sparks's *The Notebook* was filmed predominantly in the Charleston area, and you can channel your inner Noah and Allie romance by visiting many of the sites that were featured in the movie. In Mount Pleasant, follow in their footsteps by walking down historic Pitt Street to the Old Village Post House for a scoop of ice cream. Boone Hall, one of America's oldest plantations, served as the exterior of Allie's summer home, while many of the canoe scenes took place down at the creek. Downtown, the magnificent Calhoun Mansion was used for the interior scenes at Allie's home. Take a stroll through the Cistern Yard at the College of Charleston, where Allie's college scenes were filmed. And the American Theater was the scene of their first date.

Old Village Post House
101 Pitt St., Mount Pleasant
843-388-8935
oldvillageposthouseinn.com

Boone Hall Plantation
1235 Long Point Rd., Mount Pleasant
843-884-4371
boonehallplantation.com

Calhoun Mansion
16 Meeting St.
843-722-8205
calhounmansion.net

Cistern Yard at the College of Charleston
Center of campus, 66 George St.

The American Theater
446 King St., 843-853-1810
pphgcharleston.com

SPORTS AND RECREATION

WALK (OR RUN) THE
ARTHUR RAVENEL JR. BRIDGE

Built in 2005 to replace the obsolete Grace Memorial Bridge, the Arthur Ravenel Jr. Bridge is a cable-stayed bridge across the Cooper River that connects downtown Charleston to Mount Pleasant. With a total length of 13,200 feet and a main span of 1,546 feet between two diamond-shaped towers, the eight-lane bridge sports a bicycle and pedestrian path along the south edge of the bridge. With stunning views of the historic Charleston Harbor and the Atlantic Ocean, the path—known as Wonders' Way in memory of Garrett Wonders, who was killed in a biking accident while training for the 2004 Olympics—has become a playground for walkers, runners, and cyclists morning to night, while the busy weekends have their own party vibe.

US 17 between Charleston and Mount Pleasant

EXTRA CREDIT
The Arthur Ravenel Jr. Bridge is home to the annual 10K Cooper River Bridge Run—known by the locals simply as the Bridge Run—which attracts up to fifty thousand people the first weekend of April.
bridgerun.com

TAKE A CARNIVAL CRUISE

As the only cruise line offering year-round cruises out of Charleston, Carnival Cruise Line operates convenient and varied voyages from Union Pier downtown. Four- to ten-day cruises aboard the refurbished *Carnival Ecstasy* to the Bahamas and the Caribbean include ports of call like Nassau and Freeport in the Bahamas, Grand Turk in the Turks & Caicos, and "private island" ports like Princess Cays, Amber Cove, and Half Moon Cay. Though the ship could change in future years as Carnival Cruise Line shifts ships to meet market demand, the *Carnival Ecstasy* includes features like a massive WaterWorks aqua park, Serenity adults-only retreat, luxurious Spa Carnival health and wellness facilities, and lots of bars and dining options—including Guy's Burger Joint, a free-of-charge poolside venue developed in partnership with Food Network personality Guy Fieri.

196 Concord St., 800-764-7419
carnival.com

TIP
Several area hotels offer "Stay and Cruise" packages that can save big bucks on parking during a cruise.
charlestoncvb.com/special-offers/packages/stay

SEE THE GREATEST FEMALE TENNIS STARS
AT THE VOLVO CAR OPEN

The Volvo Car Open, the oldest Women's Tennis Association (WTA) professional women's tournament, is held every April at the Family Circle Tennis Center on Daniel Island. Created in 1973 and moved to Charleston in 2001, the tournament is the largest women's-only tennis tournament in North America, with a purse of $750,000, and draws more than one hundred of the world's greatest athletes, including past champions Serena Williams, Sloane Stephens, and Daria Kasatkina. The weeklong event also draws more than ninety thousand spectators to see records broken and memories made with a wide variety of other activities, including shopping in the merchandise tent, tasting unique Charleston cuisine at on-site dining locations, visiting sponsor booths offering prizes and giveaways, and checking out family fun zones, live music, pickleball clinics, and interactive tennis challenges.

161 Seven Farms Dr., 843-856-7900
volvocaropen.com

FUN FACT
Since the inception of the Volvo Car Open (previously called the Family Circle Cup) in 1973, Chris Evert has won the most tournaments with a total of eight wins.

SPEND A SPORTY WEEKEND
ON KIAWAH ISLAND

Thanks to an array of activities and amenities, ten-thousand-acre Kiawah Island (pronounced "Kee-a-Wah") is a great destination for a sporty weekend. Situated less than thirty miles from downtown Charleston, Kiawah Island Golf Resort features many sporty options, including five championship golf courses; a world-class tennis center; three swimming pool complexes; varied nature programs; stand-up paddleboarding, kayaking, and fishing; biking; a large fitness center; the garden-themed Spa at the Sanctuary (don't miss the Kiawah Golf Ball Massage); and ten miles of beaches. During the summer months, Monday night oyster roasts and sunset cruises at serene Mingo Point are very popular (oyster shucking in the Lowcountry is considered a sport), making it tempting to extend the weekend. From the luxurious Sanctuary to private homes and villas, sporty accommodation options abound.

One Sanctuary Beach Dr., 800-768-2121
kiawahresort.com

EAT, DRINK, & BOWL
AT THE ALLEY

Situated just off Upper King Street, the Alley is a bustling bowling alley that just happens to have fantastic food and drink, lots of TVs for sports fans, and arcade games and more for kids and kids at heart. The Alley features eight bowling lanes at the back of the building, plus three bars with craft beers and creative bartenders, a full kitchen sending out American classics, retro arcade games (think pinball, air hockey, and Pac-Man), two huge projection screens, and lots of TVs. The Alley hosts lots of groups and parties (including a private event space with catering), plus a schedule of special events like "Light up the Lanes" (a DJ dance party with lights, lasers, and bowling), other parties, performances, and more.

131 Columbus St., 843-818-4080
thealleycharleston.com

TIP
Locals know the Alley has nicely priced weekly food, drink, bowling, and arcade specials.

GO PADDLING
WITH COASTAL EXPEDITIONS

The Lowcountry features dozens of creeks and other waterways best explored by kayak and other small boats. Mount Pleasant–based Coastal Expeditions makes it easy to go paddling—and more. Half-day kayak tours feature naturalist guides, with frequent wildlife sightings including pelicans, dolphins, and ospreys, as well as the possibility of turtles and manatees. Like several Coastal Expeditions offerings, these tours leave from the flagship campus on Shem Creek in Mount Pleasant, as well as from the Folly Creek (Folly Beach) and Isle of Palms outposts. Full-day tours can go further afield to blackwater and inland waterways or out to barrier islands. Other offerings include stand-up paddleboard (SUP) tours, kayak and SUP rentals, boat tours and private charters, camping expeditions, and more.

514 Mill St., Mount Pleasant, 843-884-7684
2223 Folly Rd., Folly Beach, 843-406-0640
50 41st St., Isle of Palms, 843-886-9590
coastalexpeditions.com

EXTRA CREDIT

Though it's not for everyone, remote Bulls Island is a nature lover's dream destination, including lots of wildlife, sixteen miles of remote trails and road, and seven miles of undeveloped shoreline. Coastal Expeditions runs ferries and guided trips there.

SOOTHE THE SOUL
AT A SPA

There's something about a soothing spa visit that makes a day in Charleston even more civilized. Men and women in search of a unique spa experience should go to one of Stella Nova's two locations. Along with lots of salon offerings, spa services include massages, wraps, scrubs, facials, and peels. Men in search of their own soothing experience will want to head to the Old South Barber Spa, which offers classic haircuts, shaves, and more. The signature haircut includes a conditioning scalp massage and hot lather neck shave, while the old-fashioned shave is a soothing hot lather straight blade shave, including hot towels. There are also various massages, hand and foot treatments, packages, memberships, and more. All services come with a complimentary beverage and shoe shine.

Stella Nova Spa Salon & Beauty Boutique
1320 Theater Dr., Mount Pleasant, 843-884-3838
2048 Sam Rittenberg Blvd., West Ashley, 843-766-6233
stella-nova.com

Old South Barber Spa
10 State St., 843-727-4646
oldsouthbarberspa.com

HOTEL SPAS
WELCOMING NON-GUESTS

Spa Adagio at the Francis Marion Hotel
387 King St., 843-577-2444
francismarionhotel.com

The Spa at Belmond Charleston Place
205 Meeting St., 843-937-8522
belmond.com

The Spa at Wentworth Mansion
149 Wentworth St., 888-757-1106
wentworthmansion.com

The Spa at the Sanctuary
1 Sanctuary Beach Dr., Kiawah Island, 843-768-2121
kiawahresort.com

Sand and Sea Salon and Spa
at Wild Dunes Resort
1 Sundial Cir., Isle of Palms, 843-886-2555
destinationhotels.com

GET OUT ON THE WATER
ON A BOAT TOUR

Of course, the waterlogged Charleston area has lots of boat tour options. In business since 1961, SpiritLine Cruises features many choices. Its popular ninety-minute Charleston Harbor Tour with live narration provides an easy way to get on the water. Departing from two locations, this tour includes lots of history and culture, plus great views of the Battery and the rest of downtown, Fort Sumter, Patriots Point and the USS *Yorktown*, the soaring Ravenel Bridge, and more. Tours depart from downtown at the South Carolina Aquarium, as well as over at Patriots Point in Mount Pleasant. Other tour options with SpiritLine cruises include dinner cruises with delectable cuisine, a full-service bar and live music; special seasonal cruises; many combo tours; and land-based exploration.

360 Concord St. (South Carolina Aquarium Wharf)
and 40 Patriots Point Rd. (Patriots Point)
Mount Pleasant, 843-722-2628
spiritlinecruises.com

SOME MORE BOAT TOUR OPTIONS

AquaSafaris
24 Patriots Point Rd., Mount Pleasant, 843-886-8133
aqua-safaris.com

Charleston Harbor Tours
10 Wharfside St., 843-722-1112
charlestonharbortours.com

Fort Sumter Tours
340 Concord St. (Liberty Square) and 40 Patriots Point Rd. (Patriots Point), Mount Pleasant
843-722-2628 or 843-883-3123
fortsumtertours.com and nps.gov/fosu

Sandlapper Water Tours
10 Wharfside St., 843-849-8687
sandlappertours.com

Schooner Pride Tall Ship
360 Concord St. (Liberty Square), 843-722-1112
schoonerpride.com

CHEER ON THE RIVERDOGS
AT THE JOE

Officially named Joseph P. Riley Jr. Park for beloved former Charleston mayor Joe Riley, "The Joe" is always ranked as one of the best professional minor league baseball stadiums in the country. With a bucolic ballpark setting that features the Ashley River beyond the outfield fence, the Joe and the Charleston RiverDogs are renowned for hosting lots of special events and giveaways that make every game much more than balls, strikes, and cheers. Bill Murray, a co-owner and the "director of fun," loves attending games and has been known to throw and catch first pitches. There's not a bad seat in the house—especially in the luxury Riley Park Club with one-of-a-kind views of all the action and Lowcountry vistas, as well as elevated ballpark dining.

360 Fishburne St., 843-577-3647
riverdogs.com

EXTRA CREDIT
Of course, food and drink is also part of ballpark fun, with the all-beef RiverDog at DogWorld featuring cole slaw, mustard BBQ sauce, and pickled okra. Other ballpark versions of Southern classics abound (like the shrimp and grits corn dog).

OTHER PRO TEAMS & EVENTS TO CHEER IN CHARLESTON

Charleston Battery
(soccer)
1990 Daniel Island Dr. (MUSC Health Stadium)
Daniel Island, 843-971-4625
charlestonbattery.com

Megadock Billfishing Tournament
(professional fishing)
17 Lockwood Dr. (Charleston City Marina)
843-278-4920
megadocktournament.com

South Carolina Stingrays
(hockey)
5001 Coliseum Dr. (North Charleston Coliseum)
North Charleston, 843-744-2248
stingrayshockey.com

Sperry Charleston Race Week
(professional sailing)
843-628-5900
charlestonraceweek.com

Volvo Car Open
(women's professional tennis tournament)
161 Seven Farms Dr. (Family Circle Tennis Center), Daniel Island,
843-856-7900
volvocaropen.com

GO CAMPING
OUT ON CAPERS ISLAND

Situated less than an hour from Charleston but a world away, deserted Capers Island, which can be reached only by boat, provides a classic primitive camping trip for the well prepared. Most campers choose to kayak there as part of the adventure, hauling in their own food, cooking system, water, sleeping bag, tent, and more. Kayakers bound for Capers Island usually launch from the Isle of Palms Marina and paddle about four-and-a-half miles to the island. Once there, hiking and fishing, plus just enjoying the incredible quiet, are popular activities. Boneyard Beach, with its huge stands of petrified trees from Hurricane Hugo and other storms, is worth the trip on its own. Coastal Expeditions and Half-Moon Outfitters can help make this unique and adventurous camping trip happen.

Coastal Expeditions
514 Mill St., Mount Pleasant, 843-884-7684
coastalexpeditions.com

Half-Moon Outfitters
425 Coleman Blvd., Mount Pleasant, 843-881-9472
halfmoonoutfitters.com

SEE CHARLESTON
BY BIKE

Cycling is a great way to truly explore a city and get healthy at the same time. Charleston's bike share program—appropriately named Holy Spokes—makes it easier than ever to get around the Holy City. With upwards of 250 bikes available at more than two dozen different bike rack locations around the peninsula, riders can rent bikes 24/7 for eight dollars per hour (the program also offers monthly and annual rates). The adorable turquoise bikes are perfect for point-to-point destinations, long scenic rides, or simply to explore Charleston's nooks and crannies. There's even a "hold" feature that lets you stop for up to thirty minutes and, when you are done, just return it to any bike rack. And it can all be done from your smartphone.

charlestonbikeshare.com

FUN FACT

The Holy Spokes lightweight aluminum bikes have waterproof Kevlar seats and puncture-resistant tires and even track your calories burned, carbon dioxide emissions reduced, and money saved versus driving through the mobile app or on the website. So you can feel clean and green as you cycle.

TAKE A SURFING LESSON

With lots of Atlantic Ocean beachfront and waves just minutes from downtown, it's not surprising that many companies offer surfing lessons throughout the area. From group lessons to private one-on-one tutoring for any level of surfer (including many first-timers), it's easy to find the perfect lesson. The programs and offerings are quite varied, and it's simply a matter of spending time online, on the phone, and possibly in person to find the best fit. Lessons may include video instruction, classroom time, beach work (learning how to paddle out, sitting and kneeling, standing up, and more), and time in the water (with in-water instruction and, often, gentle pushes to get you going). There's nothing like that first time riding a wave—even if it's just for a few seconds.

Surf lessons are available at Folly Beach, the Isle of Palms, Sullivan's Island, Kiawah Island, and Seabrook Island. Some companies start their lessons at one of their shops, while others start right at the beach.

Carolina Salt Surf Lessons, 843-452-4833, carolinasaltsurflessons.com

Charleston Surf Lessons, 843-452-5293, charlestonsurflessons.com

Folly Beach Surf Lessons, 843-230-5090, follybeachsurflessons.com

Isla Surf School, 843-813-7897, islasurfschool-charleston.com

Shaka Surf School, 843-607-9911, shakasurfschool.com

GET ZIPPY
AT CHARLESTON ZIP LINE ADVENTURES

Situated just fifteen minutes or so north of downtown on a quaint tree-filled property in the Awendaw area, Charleston Zip Line Adventures offers a range of mild to wild zip line canopy tour choices. The main zip lining option starts from a sixty-five-foot tower, with a total of seven zip lines stretching between tree towers and platforms for a total of three thousand feet. There are also three swinging bridges, and the finale is an exhilarating 750-foot zippity-doo-dah. There's a minimum age of ten for this adventure, with a minimum weight of 70 pounds and a maximum weight of 250 pounds. There's also a climbing wall, a Kids Zip course, and lots of group, team-building, and celebration (think birthday parties and more) offerings.

1152 Guerins Bridge Rd., Awendaw, 843-928-3947
charlestonziplineadventures.com

TIP
Designed for kids five to ten years old, the Kids Zip ranges in height from ground level to about twenty-five feet, with a circuit for beginners and one for the more adventurous. Parents can go on the Big Zip Line Canopy Tour while their little ones stay down on the kid's course. Reservations must be made in advance.

SMELL THE ROSES
AT HAMPTON PARK

There is so much to do in Charleston that sometimes it can feel a bit overwhelming. Sometimes you just have to stop and smell the roses. And there's no better place to do that than Hampton Park. Bordered by the Citadel to the west and the sought-after neighborhoods of Hampton Park Terrace, Wagener Terrace, and North Central, this sixty-acre public park is the largest on the peninsula and features one of the most extensive floral displays in the city. With a rose collection and seasonal beds maintained by volunteers and indigenous trees and shrubs, the park is a natural arboretum and makes for a perfect picnic spot. The one-mile trail around the perimeter welcomes walkers, joggers, and cyclists, and the park hosts events, family reunions, and weddings.

30 Mary Murray Dr.

TIP
Make a day of it at Hampton Park with a picnic. Pick up soups, salads, sandwiches, or toasts at nearby Park Cafe (730 Rutledge Ave.). theparkcafechs.com

GO CLIMB A WALL

Except for the Arthur Ravenel Jr. Bridge, a few tall buildings, and some other man-made structures, Charleston and the Lowcountry aren't known for elevated heights much above ground level. However, the Climbing Wall at James Island County Park offers a great way to gain some elevation. At fifty feet, the Climbing Wall is one of the tallest in the Lowcountry and features more than 4,500 square feet of climbing space, with fourteen top ropes and two lead climbing walls offering challenges for all levels of experience, including complete beginners. Staff is on hand to help with safety procedures for all abilities and ages. Also part of the Outdoor Zone at James Island County Park are a ten-foot Bouldering Wall and the Rock Shop, featuring great climbing gear and accessories.

871 Riverland Dr., 843-795-4386
charlestoncountyparks.com

EXTRA CREDIT

Popular James Island County Park also features a campground and vacation cottages, a dog park, and lots of trails and views, as well as fishing; bike, pedal boat, and kayak rentals; the Splash Zone Waterpark; the Challenge Course; and more.

WALK ON WATER
WITH SUP SAFARIS

Exploring Charleston on the water is one of the best ways to get up close and personal with the unique salt marsh ecosystems of the area waterways, see indigenous wildlife, and get buff all at the same time. Charleston SUP Safaris in Folly Beach is your SUP headquarters, offering dolphin safaris, Morris Island Lighthouse tours, flatwater (river) and surf (beach) lessons, SUP yoga and fitness classes (yep, it's on a paddleboard), SUP races and special events with 10K, 5K, kids' races and even tandem dog races, and paddleboard rentals—by the hour, daily, or weekly, and they'll even deliver. Stand-up paddleboarding makes for great group activities and wedding parties. And if you become a SUP convert, they can even sell you one through their extensive sales program.

83 Center St., Folly Beach, 843-817-7877
charlestonsupsafaris.com

BE A BEACH BUM
AT FOLLY BEACH

A day on Folly Beach, just fifteen miles from downtown, is like a time warp and a throwback to simpler times. Snuggled on a narrow strip of land between the Folly River and the Atlantic Ocean, Folly Beach marches to its own tune with a laid-back vibe and friendly energy. With six miles of wide beaches, a one-thousand-foot fishing pier with a tackle shop and a full-service seafood restaurant, and an eclectic beach town community, it's the perfect beach day trip. Whether you prefer sunning, surfing, and swimming or crabbing, fishing, or waterskiing, it can all be found beachside. And just a few steps from the beach, downtown Folly is full of funky shops, surf shops, casual cafés, seafood restaurants, dive bars, one-of-a-kind clubs, and live music at every turn.

Folly Beach is located fifteen miles south of the peninsula and is accessible by car via Route 17 to Route 171 to the "Edge of America."

visitfolly.com

TIP
Folly Beach can get busy in the summer months. Your best bet is to go early or late in the day. Paid parking is plentiful along West Ashley Road, and there is one wheelchair access ramp at 9th Street on West Ashley.

GET HORSEY
AT SEABROOK ISLAND

The Equestrian Center at Seabrook Island offers several unique ways to get horsey in the Charleston area. Seabrook Island is about forty-five minutes from downtown and is considered a classic Lowcountry island and beach. It has long been enjoyed as an ideal island getaway for locals and those from further afield. The Equestrian Center is best known for offering horseback rides on three miles of trails along the beach, for everyone from beginners to more advanced riders—making it a great way to get horsey on the beach. The Equestrian Center also offers pony rides and more to kids and families, leisurely guided trail rides, guided walking rides, advanced beach rights, and private lessons. Reservations are required for all offerings.

2313 Seabrook Island Rd., Johns Island, 843-768-7541
seabrookisland.com

EXTRA CREDIT

Those with their own horse or access to one should head to Mullet Hall Equestrian Center at Johns Island County Park (2662 Mullet Hall Rd., Johns Island, 843-762-9965). It offers twenty miles of pretty riding trails that are also great for walkers. Though there are many other horsey offerings at the popular facility, it does not feature riding lessons, rentals, or boarding.

charlestoncountyparks.com.

GET FIT AND CELEBRATE LIFE
WITH DRAGON BOATING

Dragon boat racing is all the rage and one of the fastest-growing team water sports in the world. Originating in China more than two thousand years ago, dragon boats generally consist of twenty paddlers sitting two abreast in festive forty-eight-foot vessels while paddling to the beat of a drummer. Dragon Boat Charleston was founded in 2003 with the mission of promoting physical and mental wellness among cancer survivors and the community. DBC members can be seen practicing almost every night of the week along the Ashley River preparing for the five to six races they compete in annually, getting a workout, or simply enjoying an evening sunset. Join DBC as a paddler or simply watch the racing as a spectator sport while supporting a worthy cause.

dragonboatcharleston.org

TIP
Watch the nightly practices at Brittlebank Park along the Ashley River.

EXTRA CREDIT

Unleash your inner dragon at the
culmination of the DBC year with the
Charleston Dragon Boat Festival held every
May on the banks of the Ashley River.
One of the largest dragon boat festivals in the
country, it is an inspiring celebration of cancer
survivors with a fierce and fun competition, a
huge party, creative costumes, colorful tents,
and food and fun for everyone.

charlestondragonboatfestival.com

CATCH THE BIG ONE

Since Charleston is so water focused, there are lots of fishing opportunities inshore, offshore, and out in the deep sea. And chartering a boat makes it easy to go fish. Among many possibilities, The Reel Deal Charters offers a wide variety of charter fishing options. The company specializes in saltwater fishing near and far, including sea bass, sheepshead, shark, red drum, speckled sea trout, flounder, porgy, triggerfish, king mackerel, sailfish, wahoo, tuna, mahi, and more. Reel Deal offers a range of boats and charter trips, including inshore, nearshore, offshore trolling, and offshore bottom fishing. It has minimums and maximums for the different charter trips and will work with individuals to pair them with others to meet the minimum for the trip.

545 Hidden Blvd. (multiple pickup locations), Mount Pleasant
843-388-5093
thereeldealcharters.com

TIP

For those who like to eat what they catch, fish cleaning is normally available on charters. It's typically charged by the pound and includes filleting and packaging. Many charter companies also work with local restaurants to provide "you catch, we cook."

OTHER CHARTER FISHING CONTACTS

All in One Charters
1407 Shrimp Boat Ln., Mount Pleasant, 843-330-3272
allinonecharters.com

AquaSafaris
24 Patriots Point Rd., Mount Pleasant, 843-886-8133
aqua-safaris.com

Charleston Fishing Charters
4 Ashley Point Dr. (Ripley Light Marina), 704-999-6597
fishingcharterscharlestonsc.com

Charleston Sport Fishing
1610 Ben Sawyer Blvd. (Toler's Cove Marina)
Mount Pleasant, 843-860-1664
50 41st Ave. (Isle of Palms Marina), Isle of Palms
843-860-1664
charlestonsportfishing.com

RedFin Charters
145 Lockwood Dr., 843-277-5255
bestinshorefishingcharters.com

The Charleston Angler
1113 Market Center Blvd., Mount Pleasant
843-884-2095
654 St. Andrews Blvd., West Ashley, 843-571-3899
thecharlestonangler.com

Therapy Fishing Charters
843-872-8020
therapyfishing.com

CULTURE AND HISTORY

GET A GLIMPSE OF OLD CHARLESTON
IN A HISTORIC HOME

It's easy to see old Charleston by taking a tour of the many historic homes and house museums to see how genteel Charlestonians lived as the city was developing. From homes that were significant during the American Revolution and housed signers of the Declaration of Independence (Heyward-Washington House) to homes that have been preserved to depict life in the nineteenth century, including slave quarters and carriage houses (Aiken-Rhett House), and homes that have been restored to show how the moneyed founding fathers lived (Joseph Manigault House, Nathaniel Russell House, Calhoun Mansion, and Edmondston-Alston House), a tour of any historic home will be an education in architectural styles and period home furnishings—leaving you with a deeper understanding of how Charleston developed through the years.

Heyward-Washington House
87 Church St., 843-722-0354
charlestonmuseum.org

Nathaniel Russell House Museum
51 Meeting St., 843-724-8481
historiccharleston.org

Aiken-Rhett House Museum
48 Elizabeth St., 843-723-1159
historiccharleston.org

Joseph Manigault House
350 Meeting St., 843-723-2926
charlestonmuseum.org

Calhoun Mansion
16 Meeting St., 843-722-8205
calhounmansion.net

Edmondston-Alston House
21 E Battery St., 843-722-7171
edmondstonalston.com

HELP SOLVE THE MYSTERY
OF THE *HUNLEY* SUBMARINE

The *Hunley* submarine played a major role in the Civil War during the blockade of Charleston Harbor and in 1864 became the first successful combat submarine in world history when she attacked and sank the USS *Housatonic*, a major ship in the Union's fleet. Afterward, she mysteriously vanished and was lost at sea for more than a century. After searching for the remains for decades, she was finally found in 1995 and painstakingly raised and brought to the Warren Lasch Conservation Center in North Charleston for restoration and preservation. Today, the mystery of the *Hunley* can be explored during weekend tours featuring docent-led inspection of the actual submarine (on display in a 75,000-gallon conservation tank), a full-sized replica, artifacts found inside the crew compartment, interactive displays, submarine history, and a gift store.

1250 Supply St., 843-743-4865, hunley.org

TIP
Private group tours of twenty or more guests can be scheduled on weekdays between 9 a.m. and 5 p.m. when scientists may be working to preserve the *Hunley* for future generations.

STROLL THROUGH HISTORY
AT MAGNOLIA CEMETERY

Magnolia Cemetery, on the banks of the Cooper River just north of downtown, was founded in 1849 and remains the oldest public cemetery in Charleston. It has been listed on the National Register of Historic Places as a historic district since 1978. As one of the country's most beautiful examples of Victorian cemetery design, it has hosted more than thirty thousand burials and serves as the final resting place for dozens of South Carolina's founding fathers, senators, governors, and members of Charleston's illustrious literary and artist community, as well as the remains of the *Hunley* submarine crew, Confederate soldiers, and the only Egyptian pyramid mausoleum in the state. Its peaceful and bucolic grounds feature lush landscape, paths, and ponds and offer a spiritual stroll through the history of the Holy City.

70 Cunnington Ave., 843-722-8638
magnoliacemetery.net

PLUNGE INTO
PATRIOTS POINT NAVAL
& MARITIME MUSEUM

It's only natural that the water-focused Charleston area would have a museum devoted to seafaring history. Patriots Point Naval & Maritime Museum is South Carolina's most-visited heritage attraction for good reason, thanks to the presence of the huge USS *Yorktown* aircraft carrier, the USS *Laffey* destroyer, the USS *Clamagore* submarine, more than two dozen aircraft, and so much more. It's the fourth-largest naval museum in the country and one of only two with more than two ships. Other highlights of a visit can include the Medal of Honor Museum and the Vietnam Experience, which simulates a "brown water" Navy support base and a US Marine Corps artillery firebase. Active duty military members in uniform receive free admission and those with their ID cards get a discount.

40 Patriots Point Rd., 843-619-7529
patriotspoint.org

TIP
Even veteran Patriots Point visitors may not know of the USS *Yorktown* camping program, where youth groups of ten or more can sleep in bunks, eat in the mess hall, watch movies, and more. Participation requirements are generally easy to meet.

EXPLORE WHERE THE CIVIL WAR STARTED
AT FORT SUMTER

The nation's bloodiest war began at Fort Sumter on April 12, 1861, when Confederate forces fired on the Union-held stronghold. This started the American Civil War. Fort Sumter is a unit of the National Park Service (NPS) and is located on a man-made island at the entrance to Charleston Harbor. Fort Sumter Tours is the official NPS concessioner operating the ferry service for the fort. Boat tours leave from downtown Charleston and Mount Pleasant's Patriots Point. The ferry schedule varies depending on the time of the year. Purchasing tickets in advance online is highly recommended. All trips include a guided harbor tour, and trips typically last two hours and fifteen minutes, including an hour at Fort Sumter—where there is an extensive museum and store and national park rangers provide presentations.

340 Concord St. (Liberty Square) and 40 Patriots Point Rd. (Patriots Point)
Mount Pleasant, 843-883-3123
fortsumtertours.com and nps.gov/fosu

EXTRA CREDIT
Fort Sumter Tours participants should be sure to leave time before or after the trip to explore the excellent Fort Sumter museum at the Liberty Square departure point or at Patriots Point (separate ticket purchase required to visit Patriots Point).

LAND
AT CHARLES TOWNE LANDING
STATE HISTORIC SITE

Situated on bucolic Lowcountry marshland near the Ashley River across from downtown, Charles Towne Landing marks the spot where a small group of English settlers landed in 1670 to begin the establishment of the Carolina colony. Now part of the impressive South Carolina State Parks system, the sprawling state historic site devoted to early South Carolina Colonial history features a visitor center with a twelve-room exhibit hall and hands-on exhibits, a self-guided history trail (nicely narrated audio tours available), the Adventure (a replica of the seventeenth-century trading ship used by the first settlers), the Animal Forest natural habitat zoo, burial sites and cemeteries, and sprawling gardens that include a stunning live oak allée and the Legare-Waring House, which is a classic representation of an antebellum plantation home and a popular wedding site.

1500 Old Towne Rd., 843-852-4200
southcarolinaparks.com

EXPLORE
AFRICAN AMERICAN CULTURE AND HISTORY AT MCLEOD PLANTATION HISTORIC SITE

Located on James Island, just west of downtown, McLeod Plantation Historic Site was the location of nearly three hundred years of continuous agricultural use. The thirty-seven-acre former sea island cotton plantation features an outstanding collection of historic buildings, several oak allées, and a rich archaeological record. The most significant aspect of the site is its connection to enslaved Africans and their efforts to achieve freedom and social equality. At the height of the plantation's cotton production, as many as one hundred enslaved African Americans lived there. Transition Row, which features six houses built for the enslaved at McLeod, was home to generations of African Americans from the 1850s through the 1980s. The stories of these people and their daily lives are the main focus of the site.

325 Country Club Dr., 843-795-4386
charlestoncountyparks.com

EXTRA CREDIT
After the Civil War, the main house served as a regional office for the Freedmen's Bureau, and Transition Row provided homes to freedmen and their families.

TEND TURTLES
AT THE SOUTH CAROLINA AQUARIUM

With an expansive coastline, South Carolina is home to an enormous population of sea turtles from spring to fall. And with that comes the issue of sick or injured turtles. Since 2000, the South Carolina Aquarium has been tending to the health and well-being of the state's turtle population in its Sea Turtle Hospital. Visitors can be a part of the recovery efforts in the Sea Turtle Care Center™ and Zucker Family Sea Turtle Recovery™. This experience brings the daily operations of the rescue, rehabilitation, and release of the turtles to the first floor, with five galleries showcasing each stage of recovery. Visitors can test their skills at triage, peer into the surgery room, come face to face with the patients, and be part of the care for these amazing endangered species.

100 Aquarium Wharf, 843-577-3474
scaquarium.org

TIP
Although any time is a great time to visit the aquarium, you'll find smaller crowds on weekdays before 11 a.m. and after 2 p.m.

GET ARTSY
AT THE GIBBES MUSEUM OF ART

Since opening its doors back in 1905, the Gibbes Museum of Art has been the go-to place in Charleston to get artsy. The permanent collection now spans four centuries and focuses on America and the American South. There are paintings, sculptures, works on paper, decorative arts, multimedia, and more. The permanent collection also includes more than six hundred tiny portrait miniatures, which are typically painted in watercolors on thin ivory disks. America's first portrait miniatures were painted locally. The Gibbes also hosts many temporary exhibits, programs, lectures, workshops, classes, and special events. Even regular visitors and Gibbes Museum members may not know that free (with admission) docent-led public tours are held at 2:30 p.m., Tuesday to Friday, and the second Sunday of each month, as well as on Wednesdays at 5:30 p.m.

135 Meeting St., 843-722-2706
gibbesmuseum.org

WORSHIP THE CHURCHES
OF THE HOLY CITY

Everywhere you turn in Charleston, you'll see a horizon filled with steeples and spires, and you will hear a symphony of church bells on Sundays. Since the city is home to more than four hundred places of worship of different denominations, an exploration of some of the city's most historic churches and synagogues gives an insight into the history of religious tolerance and an understanding why it's called The Holy City. From the oldest Unitarian church in the South to a classic example of Romanesque architecture at the Circular Congregational Church, the country's second oldest synagogue at Kahal Kadosh Beth Elohim, and the oldest black congregation south of Baltimore and the site of the tragic 2015 shooting at Emanuel AME Church, Charleston's religious inspiration can be found on every block.

TIP
The Circular Congregational Church was founded by the original Charles Towne settlers in 1681 and houses the city's oldest graveyard, with monuments dating from 1695.

The city has dozens of notable churches due to their age or architectural grandeur. Here is a list of some of the most significant churches that are still active houses of worship and are open to the public
(in alphabetical order):

Circular Congregational Church
150 Meeting St., 843-577-6400
circularchurch.org

Emanuel AME Church
110 Calhoun St., 843-722-2561
emanuelamechurch.org

French Huguenot Church
136 Church St., 843-722-4385
huguenot-churgh.org

Kahal Kadosh Beth Elohim Synagogue
90 Hassell St., 843-723-1090
kkbe.org

St. Michael's Church
Corner of Meeting St. and Broad St., 843-723-0603
stmichaelschurch.net

St. Philip's Church
142 Church St., 843-722-7734
stphilipschurchsc.org

Unitarian Church of Charleston
4 Archdale St., 843-723-4617
charlestonuu.org

MARCH OFF
TO A CITADEL DRESS PARADE

The Citadel was established in 1842 and was originally located on Marion Square downtown (today's Embassy Suites by Hilton Charleston Historic District). Dress parades typically take place every Friday afternoon at 3:45 p.m. from September to May, but it's best to call ahead or go online to confirm there's a parade. Dating back to Alexander the Great in Europe and Valley Forge in the United States, parades and reviews are meant to foster esprit de corps, inspect troops, render honors, and preserve long traditions. Today, Citadel dress parades are often used to present awards and recognize students, faculty, staff, and other notables. A visit to the Citadel Museum and a tour of the campus will help put the parade and the unique place in perspective.

171 Moultrie St., 843-325-2294
citadel.edu

STAY IN THE OLD CITADEL

The Citadel has not always been on the banks of the Ashley River. It was originally established in downtown Charleston on today's Marion Square in a building that is now the 153-room Embassy Suites by Hilton Charleston Historic District. Built in 1829, the building was originally an arsenal. It became the Citadel Academy in 1843. During the Civil War, Union troops took over the building, with the school closing in 1865. It reopened in 1882 and remained open until 1922, when the Citadel was moved to its current campus. Today's visitors and hotel guests can walk on preserved wood floors and pass through arches once used by cadets. Artifacts, including bullets, buttons, books, and more are on display in the lobby.

337 Meeting St., 843-723-6900
embassysuites.com

REVEL IN CHARLESTON'S BEAUTY
THROUGH ITS IRONWORK

Much of Charleston's beauty comes from the stunning wrought ironwork found throughout the city. Some are original eighteenth-century works, but many were created in the twentieth century by one man. Philip Simmons (1912–2009) was a Charleston artisan and blacksmith who spent his entire adult life creating ironworks. He is responsible for more than five hundred decorative ornamental wrought iron gates, fences, balconies, and window grills. Some say that the city of Charleston is truly decorated by his hand from end to end. His work can be found throughout the city at private homes, churches, alleyways, and public spaces, as well as at the Philip Simmons Museum House—where most of his works were created—and the Philip Simmons Memorial Garden behind St. John's Reformed Episcopal Church.

Philip Simmons Museum House
30½ Blake St.
philipsimmons.us

Philip Simmons Memorial Garden
St. John's Reformed Episcopal Church
91 Anson St.

FUN FACT

Other Philip Simmons wrought iron masterpieces can be found on Daniel Island (where he was born), in the main corridor of the Charleston International Airport, and in the Governor's Mansion in Columbia, as well as in the Atlanta History Center, the Museum of International Folk Art in Santa Fe, and the Smithsonian Institute's National Museum of American History.

STAY IN A MANSION

Wentworth Mansion's long history makes it a must-stay for history and luxury buffs looking to live like a friend of a Charleston mansion owner. Built in 1886, Wentworth Mansion is the former home of a cotton merchant. Current owner Richard Widman carefully restored the mansion in 1998, converting it into an upscale boutique hotel. Each room and suite features gaslit fireplaces with original marble mantels, king-size sleigh beds, inlaid design floors, whirlpool tubs, and walk-in showers. Guests can also enjoy watching the sunset from the hotel's rooftop cupola, a special spot with 360-degree views of the city and harbor. In addition to complimentary afternoon wine and hors d'oeuvres, guests are invited to Circa 1886, the award-winning restaurant housed in the mansion's carriage house, for a gourmet breakfast.

149 Wentworth St., 877-795-4266
wentworthmansion.com

EXTRA CREDIT

Executive chef Marc Collins's refined cuisine makes dinner at Circa 1886 a sumptuous addition to any stay. Its "5 for 5 at 5" from 5 p.m. to 7 p.m., Monday to Saturday, is a fine way to start the evening, with five specialty cocktails and five wines available for just five dollars at the bar or out in the lush patio garden.
circa1886.com

GET SPOOKED
ON A GHOST TOUR

Based on Julian T. Buxton III's best-selling book, *The Ghosts of Charleston*, Tour Charleston's eighty-minute evening Ghosts of Charleston walking tour departs from Buxton Books near the Cooper River. The store has been offering ghost tours since 1996 and the tour remains the oldest ghost tour in the city. Theatrical guides weave stories about the headless Confederate soldier haunting the Battery, various unexplained occurrences on the Cooper River Bridge, the East Bay specter, Edgar Allan Poe's time in Charleston, and more. The tour also includes a visit to the lush Unitarian Church graveyard, which was built in 1772 and holds many haunted tales, including the luminescent Lady in White, who wanders through the cemetery's thick foliage. Be sure to pick up a copy of Buxton's book to relive the experience.

2A Cumberland St., 843-723-1670
tourcharleston.com

TIP
On many mornings, Tour Charleston offers its popular Lost Stories of Black Charleston, based on another book and hosted by the multitalented author, historian, and licensed tour guide Damon Fordham. Be sure to ask about other tour options.

PLAN A PARADE
OF PLANTATIONS

Rich in history and steeped in tradition, Charleston plantations are a window into what life was like in the pre–Civil War South. Boone Hall Plantation was a major cotton-producing estate covering more than 17,000 acres and, in addition to plantation and garden tours, it hosts compelling slave history and Gullah culture tours. A tour of Drayton Hall is more a study of its circa-1738 building design as one of the nation's earliest examples of Palladian architecture. Home to the Drayton family and still owned by a twelfth-generation descendant, Magnolia Plantation is all about the informal English-style gardens and is the oldest public garden in America. Middleton Place combines many elements of plantation life and brings the house museum collections, geometric patterned-landscaped gardens, and artistry of craftspeople to life.

Boone Hall Plantation
1235 Long Point Rd., Mount Pleasant, 843-884-4371
boonehallplantation.com

Drayton Hall Plantation
3380 Ashley River Rd., 843-769-2600, draytonhall.org

Magnolia Plantation
3550 Ashley River Rd., 843-571-1266, magnoliaplantation.com

Middleton Place
4300 Ashley River Rd., 843-556-6020, middletonplace.org

TIP

For a true immersion into plantation life, don't miss Plantation Days at Middleton Plantation one weekend every November, when craftsmen demonstrate skills practiced by slaves as they prepared the plantation for winter, including activities like cane pressing, spinning, brickmaking, leather tanning, and cider making. Additionally, the festivities include African American culture presentations and Gullah storytelling.

EXTRA CREDIT

Don't miss the other plantations around Charleston that are featured elsewhere.

Charles Towne Landing State Historic Site
southcarolinaparks.com/ctl

Charleston Tea Plantation
charlestonteaplantation.com

McLeod Plantation Historic Site
charlestoncountyparks.com

SEE CHARLESTON
THROUGH THE WORDS OF PAT CONROY

The late Pat Conroy waxed poetically about the Lowcountry and Charleston. *South of Broad* was his love letter to the city (calling it "the Mansion on the River"), and many of the places mentioned in the novel can be visited through his words. Some of the possibilities (all featured in *South of Broad*) include the Gibbes Museum of Art (135 Meeting Street), Mills House Hotel (115 Meeting Street), St. Michael's Church (71 Broad Street), Dock Street Theatre (135 Church Street), and pretty Legare and Water Streets. Of course, the Citadel and Charleston were the fictional settings for his earlier novel, *The Lords of Discipline*. Charleston and the Lowcountry are also featured prominently in *The Pat Conroy Cookbook: Recipes and Stories of My Life*, including classic Conroy tales revolving around food and several tasty recipes.

patconroy.com

GRAB SOME SHADE
AT ANGEL OAK

The Angel Oak tree on Johns Island ten miles from downtown is a fairy-tale-esque natural wonder that shouldn't be missed. Thought to be more than four hundred years old—and one of the oldest living organisms east of the Mississippi—the tree stands 66.5 feet tall, measures twenty-eight feet in circumference, and produces shade that covers more than seventeen thousand square feet. Its longest branch distance is more than 185 feet. It sits on land that was part of Abraham Waight's 1717 land grant and is now owned by the city of Charleston. Come and gawk for free and browse the gift shop with mugs, shirts, and cards featuring stunning photography of the tree, as well as Charleston-area food specialties and novelties for the kids (and kids at heart).

3688 Angel Oak Rd., Johns Island, 843-559-3496
angeloaktree.com

TIP
With picnic benches all around, the Angel Oak makes for a perfect picnic spot. Pick up a picnic lunch nearby at Stono Market & Tomato Shed Café.
842 Main Rd., Johns Island, 843-559-9999, stonofarmmarket.com

HOP ON A
CARRIAGE TOUR

There may not be anything more "Charleston" than a classic carriage tour of historic downtown above and below Broad Street. Narrated tours with licensed guides on carriages led by horses (and occasionally mules) who seem to know the way provide a great introduction or reintroduction to Charleston's history, culture, architecture, and more. The tours can vary a lot in terms of time, carriages used (from antique to modern), number of passengers (private tours are available), guides (from knowledgeable and animated to not so much), narration (ditto), guide attire (often period costumes), tour route (regulated by the city), and more. Booking in advance is a good idea, though checking out the offerings street-side in person gives a great feel for specific tours and companies.

TIP
Carriage tours are very popular. Go online well in advance to review the various options and to match a specific carriage tour with your interests.

CARRIAGE TOUR COMPANIES

Carolina Polo & Carriage Co.
843-577-6767
cpcc.com

Charleston Carriage Works
843-595-4879
mycharlestoncarriage.com

Classic Carriage Works
843-853-3747
classiccarriage.com

Old South Carriage Co.
843-723-9712
oldsouthcarriage.com

Palmetto Carriage Works
843-853-6125
palmettocarriage.com

TAKE A
GATEWAY WALK

From ghost walks to culinary tours to history, architecture, and more, there are more than a dozen different walking tours and companies in downtown Charleston. It's easy to research the options and pursue one or more of interest. However, one unique (and free) possibility that even longtime locals may not know about is something called the Gateway Walk. Conceived in 1930 by a Garden Club of Charleston president, this short four-block walk connects churches and churchyards with gardens, courtyards, and more. Start at St. John's Lutheran Church (the club has maps) and look for small explanatory plaques and footstone markers along the route, which includes stops in the gardens of the Gibbes Museum of Art and the Charleston Library, four churchyards, and many wrought iron gates (for which the walk is named).

5 Clifford St. (St. John's Lutheran Church)
gardenclubofcharleston.com

CHARLESTON'S DEFENSE
AT FORT MOULTRIE

For 171 years, Fort Moultrie protected Charleston from invasion. There have been three forts located here, with the first fort built out of palmetto trees and sand, inspiring the South Carolina flag and nickname of the Palmetto State. Although there are no physical remains of the first two forts, the third—first constructed in 1809 and with several visible changes through 1947—still stands. Fort Moultrie is part of Fort Sumter National Monument and is open year-round for guided and self-guided tours. The property features an orientation film and museum exhibits, and the historic fort and cannon represent different historical periods from the American Revolution through the Civil War and both World War I and World War II.

1214 Middle St., Sullivan's Island, 843-883-3123
nps.gov/fosu

FUN FACT
American author Edgar Allan Poe was stationed at Fort Moultrie—where he was known by the assumed name of Edgar A. Perry—from 1827 to 1828. His experiences on Sullivan's Island inspired several of his short stories.

TAKE FLIGHT
TO CAW CAW INTERPRETIVE CENTER

Located just a half hour or so west of downtown Charleston, the Caw Caw Interpretive Center is a wild world away from the hustle and bustle of the peninsula. Part of the Charleston County Park and Recreation Commission system, the Caw Caw Interpretive Center's grounds were once part of several rice plantations and a former tea farm. There are more than six miles of walking trails (pets and bikes not permitted), including elevated boardwalks through the wetlands and various exhibits and displays. Along with lots of waterfowl, otters, deer, alligators, and more, the Caw Caw property is known as a birding hot spot (including special bird-watching programs), with more than 250 species of birds calling it home—from warblers to kites to bald eagles.

5200 Savannah Hwy., Ravenel, 843-762-8015
charlestoncountyparks.com

LET HISTORY COME TO LIFE
AT THE OLD EXCHANGE & PROVOST DUNGEON

With its iconic Palladian architecture and imposing location at the corner of East Bay and Broad Streets, the Old Exchange & Provost Dungeon contains more history than almost any other building in Charleston. At one time the social, political, and economic hub of the city, the Exchange has served as a public market; a prison for pirates, Native Americans, and signers of the Declaration of Independence; storage for confiscated tea; and government offices, a post office, a town hall, and the site of many lavish events during George Washington's weeklong stay. Today, costumed docents lead public tours of its three floors—including the dungeon—that highlight many of these aspects of Colonial and Revolutionary history, along with tales of pirates and patriots that will entertain and inform the entire family.

122 E Bay St., 843-727-2165
oldexchange.org

IMMERSE YOURSELF
IN CHARLESTON'S DEEP AFRICAN AMERICAN ROOTS

When you consider that close to half of all enslaved Africans arrived in the United States through Charleston, it's no surprise that African American people, history, and culture are infused in the overall fabric of the city. The Old Slave Mart Museum is a great introduction to how the enslaved community arrived in Charleston. For an understanding of what early slave life was like, watch the "Exploring the Gullah Culture" presentation at Boone Hall Plantation or visit the Gullah/Geechee heritage site at McLeod Plantation Historic Site. Hear folktales that rarely make the history books with a Lost Stories of Black Charleston Tour, or explore the ironwork artistry of Philip Simmons, whose fingerprints are found throughout the city. This important African American history will come together with the opening of the International African American Museum in 2020.

Old Slave Mart Museum
6 Chalmers St., 843-958-6467
oldslavemartmuseum.com

Gullah Tour at Boone Hall Plantation
1235 Long Point Rd., Mount Pleasant, 843-884-4371
boonehallplantation.com

McLeod Plantation Historic Site
325 Country Club Dr., 843-762-9514
charlestoncountyparks.com

Lost Stories of Black Charleston with Tour Charleston
843-606-6025
tourcharleston.com

Philip Simmons
philipsimmons.us

International African American Museum
Gadsden's Wharf
iaamuseum.org

KID AROUND
AT THE CHILDREN'S MUSEUM
OF THE LOWCOUNTRY

Kids and kids at heart will love the Children's Museum of the Lowcountry, where the "power of play" makes this museum a fun place to learn a lot outside a classroom. The museum features numerous hands-on interactive experiences, with themed books featured in each one for power readers. The Art Room is the best place to start, so any masterpieces created will have time to dry before it's time to head home. Other options include the Idea Factory (design, build, and deconstruct with real tools), the Medieval Creativity Castle and Pirates! (costumes and more), Waterwise (navigate boats around a model of Charleston Harbor), the Publix Market (promoting healthy food purchases and eating), and, outside, the Kids' Garden, with seven different organic beds ready for watering, thinning, and picking.

25 Ann St., 843-853-8962
explorecml.org

EXTRA CREDIT
Though the museum sells a variety of snacks, the downtown location of colorful and tasty Cupcake DownSouth (433 King St.) is just around the corner.
freshcupcakes.com

HAVE A LOOK
AT THE ICONIC MORRIS ISLAND LIGHTHOUSE

Originally built back in 1767 as a forty-two-foot beacon at the southern end of Charleston Harbor, the Morris Island Lighthouse was replaced with a 102-foot version in 1838—which was destroyed during the Civil War. The current lighthouse was built in 1876, stands 161 feet tall, and was painted with black and white stripes over the original red brick (the black paint wore off more quickly, so it now appears red- and white-striped). Often referred to as the Old Charleston Light, it's easy to have a look at the iconic lighthouse by heading to the eastern end of Folly Beach, where a quarter-mile trail leads to a beach that overlooks the lighthouse out in the water (now about two hundred yards offshore, depending on the tide). Several narrated boat tours also pass nearby.

FUN FACT
Leaning slightly to the northeast, the lighthouse is owned by the state and is undergoing extensive preservation work through an organization called Save the Light (donations most welcome!).
savethelight.org

SHOPPING AND FASHION

SHOP AT THE CULTURAL HEART OF CHARLESTON
AT THE CITY MARKET

One of the nation's oldest public markets and possibly the oldest "shopping mall" in the United States, the four-block-long Charleston City Market is a shopper's delight and the true heartbeat of the city. With more than three hundred enterprising local vendors, the market starts in the Great Hall, an 18,300-square-foot corridor filled with micro-boutiques selling handmade wares, jewelry, art, stoneware and pottery, Charleston specialties, and tasty treats. The next three blocks are open-air sheds housing all kinds of evolving and eclectic finds, from sweetgrass baskets and palmetto roses (there are dozens of resident Gullah artists) to stoneground grits and everything in between for the perfect Charleston souvenir. The surrounding neighborhood along Market Street is filled with restaurants, walking and carriage tours, specialty shops, and hotels.

City Market is four blocks long along Market Street from
Meeting Street to E Bay St.
thecharlestoncitymarket.com

TIP

The Day Market is open every day from 9:30 a.m. until 6 p.m. except for Christmas Day. The Night Market is open Thursday, Friday, and Saturday evenings from 6:30 p.m. until 10:30 p.m. from April to December and showcases more than one hundred local artists with live entertainment.

FACT

The palmetto rose has been a Charleston symbol of everlasting love since the Civil War and is made from the fronds of the palmetto tree. Like sweetgrass baskets, the natural color variations of the plant ensure that no two roses are alike.

MAKE A STATEMENT
WITH A BRACKISH BOW TIE

Not willing to saddle his groomsmen with another set of cufflinks or a beer stein, Charlestonian Ben Ross set out to handcraft a set of turkey bow feathers into handsome bow ties for the men in his wedding party in 2007. That one gesture of thoughtfulness and creativity has morphed into a burgeoning business that combines artistry, style, and the spirit of the South. Today, Brackish bow ties are handcrafted locally by a team of fifty artisans and production assistants with hand-selected feathers that are painstakingly crafted into a sustainable work of art—and a fashionable men's accessory—where no two bow ties are exactly alike. Available in dozens of colors and patterns, these one-of-a-kind bow ties make for a unique gift or souvenir.

843-469-8833
brackishbowties.com

RETAIL SHOPS IN THE AREA TO PICK UP YOUR OWN BRACKISH BOW TIE

Charleston Preservation Society
147 King St., 843-723-2775
preservationsociety.org

Grand Bohemian Hotel
55 Wentworth St., 843-722-5711
grandbohemiancharleston.com

The Port Mercantile Retail Store in the Restoration
75 Wentworth St., 843-518-5118
therestorationhotel.com

Charleston Tuxedo
162 Wentworth St., 843-974-5938
charlestontuxedo.com

Grady Ervin & Co.
313 King St., 843-722-1776
gradyervin.com

The Charleston Angler
654 St. Andrews Blvd., 843-571-3899
1113 Market Center Blvd., Mount Pleasant, 843-884-2095
thecharlestonangler.com

Gwynn's of Mount Pleasant
916 Houston Northcutt Blvd., Mount Pleasant, 843-849-9667
gwynns.com

SeaCoast Sports and Outfitters
585 Freshfields Dr., Kiawah Island, 843-768-8486
seacoastsports.com

The Sanctuary at Kiawah Island Golf Resort
1 Sanctuary Beach Dr., Kiawah Island, 843-768-2121
kiawahresort.com

NEW MEETS OLD
AT FRITZ PORTER

Recognizing a need for an interior design space in downtown Charleston where you could find it all under one roof, designer Sarah-Hamlin Hastings opened Fritz Porter in the renovated and uber-cool Cigar Factory. Part curated antique center—representing fifteen different dealers with styles ranging from flea market chic to museum-quality, one-of-a-kind pieces—and part modern furniture showroom, the atelier also includes contemporary art with styles ranging from pastoral impressionism to surreal and abstract, boutique textiles and wallpaper, and custom lighting. Catering to the design trade as well as the homeowner with a DYI itch, Fritz Porter features unique gems from designers across the country, as well as a heavy dose of local artisans. Plus, it's the perfect spot to find that unique gift or bauble.

701 E Bay St., #106, 843-207-4804
fritzporter.com

FUN FACT
The Cigar Factory was built in 1881 as a cotton manufacturing plant and featured all the latest and greatest technology of the day, including electricity, steam heat, and fire safety systems. In 1903, it was sold to the American Cigar Company, which produced Roi-Tan and Cremo cigars over the next seventy years, rolling out more than 1.5 million cigars each day and employing as many as 1,400 workers at its high point.

DRESS LIKE A QUEEN
AT BERLIN'S FOR WOMEN

Berlin's was founded at the corner of King and Broad Streets in 1883 by Henry Berlin, who came to the United States from eastern Europe with $1.38 in his pocket. With a commitment to impeccable quality clothing and the highest level of customer service for both men's and women's apparel, Berlin's for Women—located next door to the men's shop—carries on that family fashion tradition with fourth-generation proprietor Ellen Berlin. Carrying a wide array of business and casual clothing, special occasion attire, accessories and handbags, jewelry, and shoes from top designers like Rachel Zoe, Badgley Mischka, and Nicole Miller and offering alterations and personal shopping, Berlin's for Women continues to make fashion statements and dress generations of Charlestonians and visitors.

116 King St., 843-723-5591
berlinsforwomen.com

DRESS LIKE A KING
AT M. DUMAS & SONS

M. Dumas & Sons has been dressing Charlestonians and visitors alike for more than a century and has solidified its position as the quintessential men's clothier of the Lowcountry. Originally established as a uniform shop for service jobs in 1917 by Mendel Dumas, the King Street shop expanded over the years into hunting and outdoor apparel and fully transitioned into men's apparel in the early 1990s. Today, the shop is run by third-generation family member David Dumas and has become the area's iconic men's specialty retailer, offering a wide assortment of business and casual fashions, shoes, accessories, and gifts from top-of-the-line designers and manufacturers including Hickey Freeman, Oliver Ridley, Southern Tide, Cole Hahn, and dozens more. Dress the man in your life with a visit to this Charleston fashion institution.

294 King St., 843-723-8603
mdumasandsons.com

OTHER KING STREET MEN'S CLOTHIERS WHERE YOU CAN DRESS TO IMPRESS

Ben Silver Collection
149 King St., 843-577-4556
bensilver.com

Berlin's Clothiers
114 King St., 843-722-1665
berlinsclothing.com

Grady Ervin & Co.
313 King St., 843-722-1776
gradyervin.com

Jordan Lash Charleston
305 King St., 843-804-6710
jordanlash.com

319 Men
316 King St., 843-577-8807
319menbyshaw.com

SURPRISE THAT SPECIAL SOMEONE
WITH A GIFT FROM CROGHAN'S JEWEL BOX

For more than one hundred years, the Croghan family has been embellishing Charlestonians and visitors with exquisite designer and estate jewelry, stunning antique silver, and unique gifts for all occasions. Opened by William Joseph Croghan, a hand engraver and jeweler, on the side porch of an eighteenth-century single home on King Street, the space has expanded over the years into the entire building. It is a treasure trove of fine jewelry, including rings, necklaces, bracelets, earrings, and pins, as well as estate jewelry; an extensive bridal selection of engagement rings, wedding bands, and anniversary bands; and gifts for everyone. The store also offers a wide variety of services, such as appraisals, corporate gifts, custom jewelry, engraving, and repairs. There's nothing quite like a Croghan's package under the tree or on bended knee.

308 King St., 843-723-3594
croghansjewelbox.com

SHOP CHARLESTON STYLE AND PRESERVATION
AT THE HISTORIC CHARLESTON FOUNDATION

Visitors have always enjoyed taking a little piece of Charleston home with them. Whether it's a sweetgrass basket, benne wafers, rice spoons, or a symbol of Charleston's hospitality in the form of a pineapple or palm tree, the Historic Charleston Foundation provides a perfect opportunity to find a treasure trove of Charleston Style™ designs. Since 1972, the foundation has worked with talented artisans and distinguished manufacturers to create beautiful objects that reflect the vibrant urban city or the serene spirit of the Lowcountry islands and marshes. From books and bedding to food, furniture, and fine art, the Historic Charleston Foundation captures the spirit of Charleston's architecture, gardens, and Southern hospitality. And best of all, proceeds support the ongoing preservation of Charleston for future generations.

The Shops of Historic Charleston Foundation
108 Meeting St., 843-724-8484, historiccharleston.org

Market Shop of Historic Charleston Foundation, Charleston City Market,
188 Meeting St., 843-300-4952, historiccharleston.org

Aiken-Rhett House Museum, 48 Elizabeth St., 843-723-1159
historiccharleston.org

Nathaniel Russell House Museum, 51 Meeting St., 843-724-8481
historiccharleston.org

● ●

SHOP 'TIL YOU DROP
ON KING STREET

Fashionable King Street is *the* place to shop in downtown, with something for everyone along the mile-long stretch down Charleston's historic main artery. Lower King is home to the antiques district with George C. Birlant & Co. leading the way as the oldest and largest antique shop in the Southeast, specializing in eighteenth- and nineteenth-century furniture, silver, and china. Elaborate sculptures, chandeliers, and vintage frames can be found nearby at John Pope Antiques. Middle King is the fashion district and is filled with standard favorites like Michael Kors and Lucky Brand rubbing elbows with upscale boutiques like Worthwhile and Hampden. Upper King is the up-and-coming area, loaded with design showrooms like kitchen designer SieMatic, lighting showroom Circa Lighting, and tons of culinary specialty shops like Callie's Hot Little Biscuit and Cupcake DownSouth.

TIP
Head to King Street on the second Sunday of the month for 2nd Sunday on King Street, when the city closes the street to all vehicular traffic from Calhoun to Wentworth Streets and makes it a pedestrian-only shopping paradise. Stroll from store to store browsing, eating, and drinking, with musicians on street corners and tasty sampling along the way.

George C. Birlant & Co.
191 King St., 843-722-3842, birlant.com

John Pope Antiques
180 King St., 573-230-1666, johnpopeantiques.com

Michael Kors
263 King St., 843-714-6132, michaelkors.com

Lucky Brand
273 King St., 843-534-2608, luckybrand.com

Worthwhile
268 King St., 843-723-4418, shopworthwhile.com

Hampden
314 King St., 843-724-6373, hampdenclothing.com

SieMatic Charleston
444 King St., 843-724-5838, siematic-charleston.com

Circa Lighting
426 King St., 843-937-5990, circalighting.com

Callie's Hot Little Biscuit
476½ King St., 843-737-5159, calliesbiscuits.com

Cupcake DownSouth
433 King St., 843-853-8181, freshcupcakes.com

BOOK IT
TO A BOOKSTORE

Whether it's the latest beach read or city history, Charleston is a town of readers. Several classic downtown bookstores oblige the reading habit, with many more available nearby. Boomer's Books, which opened in 1995, was purchased by longtime employee Jonathan Sanchez in 2007 and renamed Blue Bicycle Books (look for the blue bike out front). Along with used, new, and lots of regional offerings, the store hosts more than two hundred authors each year, as well as November's YALLFest, a young adult book festival. On the other side of downtown near the Cooper River, Buxton Books specializes in regionally focused fiction and nonfiction, but it has other offerings as well. Co-owner Julian T. Buxton III wrote *The Ghosts of Charleston*, and Tour Charleston ghost tours and other tours start at the store.

Blue Bicycle Books, 420 King St., 843-722-2666
bluebicyclebooks.com

Buxton Books, 2A Cumberland St., 843-834-6575
buxtonbooks.com

OTHER AREA BOOKSTORES

Barnes & Noble Booksellers
1716 Town Centre Way, Mount Pleasant, 843-216-9756
1812 Sam Rittenberg Blvd., West Ashley, 843-556-6561
7620 Rivers Ave., North Charleston, 843-572-2322
barnesandnoble.com

Books-A-Million
2150 Northwoods Blvd., Unit B8, North Charleston
843-764-2377, booksamillion.com

Charleston Southern University
Official Bookstore
(Barnes & Noble)
9200 University Blvd., North Charleston, 843-863-8017
csuniv.bncollege.com

The Citadel Official Bookstore
(Barnes & Noble)
171 Moultrie St., 843-953-5110
thecitadel.bncollege.com

College of Charleston Official Bookstore
(Barnes & Noble)
160 Calhoun St., 843-953-5518
cofc.bncollege.com

Itinerant Literate Books
(Charleston's Mobile Bookstore)
843-534-9553
itinerantliteratebooks.com

Pauline Books and Media
243 King St., 843-577-0175
pauline.org

Preservation Society of Charleston
Book & Gift Shop
147 King St., 843-723-2775
preservationsociety.org

TAKE HOME SOME SWEET SWEETGRASS BASKETS

The weaving of sweetgrass baskets has been practiced in the Lowcountry since the early eighteenth century, when Africans who were brought over to work the rice plantations made them for use in the field. After the Civil War, women began making baskets to store and serve food in their own homes and to sell them. Sweetgrass baskets today are an art form that can be found for sale along Charleston sidewalks, in the City Market, and especially along Sweetgrass Basket Makers Highway. In close to one hundred sometimes ramshackle kiosks along the sides of the road, the majestic baskets are hung with the hopes of luring passersby to stop for a true cultural souvenir—and to keep the sweetgrass basket tradition alive for future generations.

Sweetgrass baskets can be found along the Sweetgrass Basket Makers Highway on Route 17 from Mount Pleasant to Awendaw.

FUN FACT

Sweetgrass baskets are made with long bunches of sweetgrass, pine needles, and bulrush that are bound together with fiber strips from the native palmetto trees. The bunches are coiled to form a variety of shapes and sizes, so no two baskets are alike.

SUGGESTED ITINERARIES

GET OUTSIDE

Take a Gateway Walk, 114
Walk (or Run) the Arthur Ravenel Jr. Bridge, 62
Go Camping out on Capers Island, 74
See Charleston by Bike, 75
Be a Beach Bum at Folly Beach, 81

TOURS AND MORE

Eat up Charleston on a Culinary Tour, 5
Capture Fireflies on a Tipsy Tour, 22
Drink in History on the Original Pub Tour, 26
Get out on the Water on a Boat Tour, 70
Get Spooked on a Ghost Tour, 107
Hop on a Carriage Tour, 112

THE WILD SIDE

Get Crabby, 20
Go Wild at the Southeastern Wildlife Exposition, 44
Get Horsey at Seabrook Island, 82
Catch the Big One, 86
Tend Turtles at the South Carolina Aquarium, 98
Take Flight to Caw Caw Interpretive Center, 116

DRINK IT IN

Drink a PBR at the Recovery Room, 8
Have a Cup of Tea on Wadmalaw Island, 13
Celebrate Your Freedom with a Prohibition Pint at Blind Tiger Pub, 16
Hang a Dollar Bill at the Griffon, 17

ITINERARIES BY SEASON

SPRING

SUMMER

FALL

WINTER

INDEX

145